200 HALOGEN OVEN RECIPES

200

HAMLYN **ALL COLOUR COOKBOOK**

HALOGEN OVEN
RECIPES

An Hachette UK Company
www.hachette.co.uk

First published in Great Britain in 2010 by Hamlyn,
a division of Octopus Publishing Group Ltd,
Carmelite House, 50 Victoria Embankment,
London EC4Y 0DZ
www.octopusbooks.co.uk

This edition published in 2016

ISBN 978-0-600-63344-0

A CIP catalogue record for this book is available from the
British Library

Printed and bound in China

10 9 8 7 6 5 4 3 2 1

Standard level spoon measurement are used in all recipes.
1 tablespoon = one 15 ml spoon
1 teaspoon = one 5 ml spoon

Both imperial and metric measures have been given in
all recipes. Use one set of measurements only and not a
mixture of both.

Eggs should be medium unless otherwise stated. The
Department of Health advises that eggs should not be
consumed raw. This book contains dishes made with raw
or lightly cooked eggs. It is prudent for more vulnerable
people such as pregnant and nursing mothers, invalids,
the elderly, babies and young children to avoid uncooked
or lightly cooked dishes made with eggs. Once prepared
these dishes should be kept refrigerated and used promptly.

This book includes dishes made with nuts and nut
derivatives. It is advisable for customers with known allergic
reactions to nuts and nut derivatives and those who may be
potentially vulnerable to these allergies, such as pregnant
and nursing mothers, invalids, the elderly, babies and
children, to avoid dishes made with nuts and nut oils. It is
also prudent to check the labels of pre-prepared ingredients
for the possible inclusion of nut derivatives.

contents

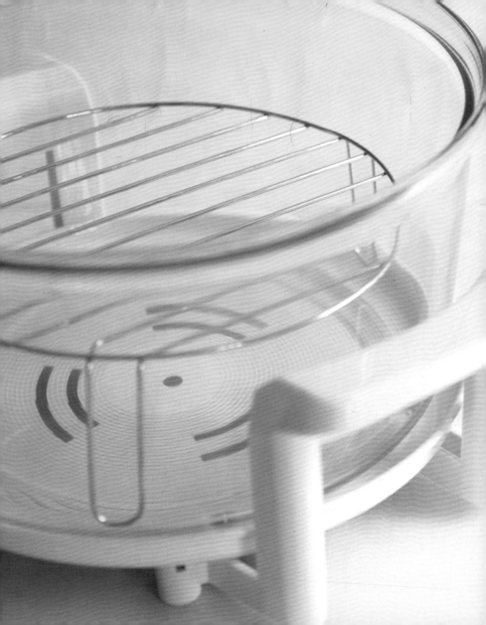

introduction

introduction

Halogen ovens have become an almost indispensable item for the modern household. Combining the convenience of a microwave oven with the desired – and delicious – outcomes that you are used to when cooking with conventional heat, they really are the ideal all-round contemporary alternative for the busy cook. If you are constantly searching for new ways to prepare tasty yet speedy meals, then a halogen oven is for you. The recipes contained here will launch you well along the path to discovering the benefits of halogen oven cooking, and you will soon wonder how you survived without one. Once you have discovered the range of simple, delicious and super-quick meals contained in these pages, you will never again need to turn to unhealthy convenience foods.

So what makes a halogen oven the kitchen appliance you just cannot live without?

the halogen promise

Long gone are the days when speedy cooking times meant soggy, unevenly cooked food from a microwave. The halogen oven promise is that it turns the outside of the food brown and crisp, and the inside of the food juicy and tender, cooking evenly throughout without any of those dreaded hot and cold spots that can mar a finished dish. Halogens ovens are also so powerful that they can cook food almost twice as fast as a conventional ovens.

And they offer many other important benefits such as saving energy and money – and even washing up! Scrumptious cakes, bakes and puddings, succulent roasted joints of meat, perfectly baked fish, homemade chips or crispy baked potatoes, stews, casseroles, risottos, pasta, pizzas – hundreds of meals can be cooked easily with impressive results.

Most halogen ovens will come with manufacturers' instructions and a handful of recipes to get you started. With such a range of choice at your disposal, however, and the added freedom you will gain from saving time in the kitchen, you will be glad of new ideas. This easy-to-use cookbook contains more than 200 recipes designed to inspire you and help you make the most of this brilliant kitchen appliance. The recipes contained here are simple but tasty, with clear step-by-step instructions, and offer a hassle-free way of cooking, whether you are creating meals for the whole family or friends, or whipping up a quick snack.

saving on every level...

A halogen oven is energy and time efficient and boasts the following unique features:

- Cooking time is cut by up to 40 per cent.
- Energy is saved in two ways: by using lower temperatures to cook and through the reduction of overall cooking time.

- Uniform heat means that food is evenly cooked with none of the hot and cold spots associated with microwave cooking.
- Juices are sealed in and food is kept moist on the inside, while the outside crisps and browns just as you would expect with a conventional oven. Food does not become soggy and dry out as can happen with even the most modern of microwave ovens.
- Fat is drained away from the tiered racks, giving you healthier dinners.
- It is portable, compact and suitable for kitchens of any size. (Why not give one to a student about to go off to university, or take it on a caravanning holiday, or to family gatherings or other occasions?)
- There is no need to defrost. Food can be cooked directly from the freezer. You can clean and season your meat, poultry or fish before freezing – then it is ready to go.
- The clear bowl allows you to monitor the results as you go along, Not only does this mean that heat (and therefore electricity) is not wasted, but also you avoid getting hot and bothered from constantly having to open the oven to check on how how your dish is progressing. There is also less need to turn the contents during cooking because everything is cooked evenly and thoroughly due to it being a fan-assisted oven.
- A halogen oven usually has a self-clean function and the glass bowl can be lifted out for wiping clean.

uniquely halogen

How does a halogen oven achieve such good results? It uses an innovative combination of powerful halogen lighting and convection currents. The infrared halogen element found in the oven heats up almost instantly. This reduces the time the oven is on prior to cooking; food also cooks evenly, without the need for turning. Using the multiple racks, or simply placing a cooking dish inside, you can cook in much the same way as a conventional oven – but much more effectively.

the basics

the halogen oven

Halogen ovens are generally supplied with the following equipment:

- 1 glass bowl
- 1 base stand
- 1 glass lid with halogen element and power cord
- 2 steel racks
- steel handles – for safe removal of racks

getting started

1 To set up the oven, place the glass bowl on the metal base (remembering to do this on a secure kitchen worktop or table).

2 The metal racks then sit one on top of the other, inside the glass bowl.

3 Next simply fit the lid onto the glass bowl and push the handle down to lock it.

4 Plug into a nearby socket. Turn the timer clockwise to select the required time. The power light will now be on.

5 Turn the temperature dial clockwise to the required temperature and the light will then come on.

6 When the oven has reached the required temperature the light will turn off.

7 The temperature will come back on again if the temperature falls and this will show that the oven is heating up again.

8 When the food is ready, (usually indicated by the bell) remove the food from the glass bowl using the steel handles.

9 The lid will now be extremely hot; therefore do NOT place it directly on your kitchen worktop.

cleaning

Many halogen ovens have a self cleaning function which can be used as follows:

1 Half-fill the glass bowl full with hot water and fit the oven's lid in place

2 Push the handle down to lock it in the correct position.

3 Set the halogen oven to the appropriate wash function.

4 Turn the timer to the required time (usually 10-15 minutes)

You should never immerse the lid in water (or any liquid). The glass bowl can be placed in your dishwasher or washed as normal and the lid can be cleaned using a damp cloth.

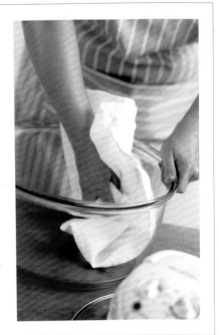

other equipment

In addition to your halogen oven, you may also need the following general kitchen equipment:.

- medium-size casserole dish
- aluminium foil
- small round baking/pizza tray
- sieve
- frying pan
- grater

- frying tray
- measuring spoons/jugs
- baking parchment
- temperature gauge/thermometer
- saucepans (various sizes)
- mixing bowls (various sizes)
- oven gloves
- clingfilm
- sharp knife
- metal/bamboo skewers

It is also possible to purchase the following equipment which is specifically for the halogen oven, from many halogen oven retailers:

• steamer pan
• frying pan
• lid stand

what food to cook?

You can cook almost any food in your halogen oven; however certain foods are more suitable.

Food can be cooked directly in the bowl or on the racks provided. It is worth noting, though, that the oven works by allowing air to circulate around the food; placing food directly in the bowl may mean increased cooking times. It is also possible to use a casserole dish or baking tray – just as you would in a conventional oven.

The following is a selection of food that can be cooked in your halogen oven:

• meat/fish/poultry
• vegetables
• pizza
• bread/cakes/pastry

Do not forget that many halogen ovens also have the ability to cook frozen food and some even have thaw functions. Remember, however, that frozen food will take longer to cook than if it were defrosted – although it will still be quicker to cook in a halogen oven than in a conventional one.

cooking times

Most halogen ovens have a lowest temperature setting of around 125°C (257°F) and a highest setting of 250°C (482°F).

You will probably notice how similar these settings are to those used when cooking with a conventional oven, the distinctive design of the halogen oven means that cooking time is vastly reduced. By moving hot air rapidly around the oven, a halogen oven cooks food evenly and quickly without hot and cold spots, and this helps to shorten the time usually needed to achieve the desired results.

temperatures and preheating

As you use the recipes from this book, you will notice that the Celsius and Fahrenheit temperatures given for cooking match what is on the temperature dial of the oven, rather than the more usual equivalents (including gas marks) that you would see in other cookbooks. You may also notice that none of the recipes within the book require you to preheat the oven. While halogen ovens can be preheated (most notably for baking cakes or puddings), the recipes here have been written and the cooking times adjusted so that preheating is unnecessary. You simply assemble and prepare the ingredients as directed, put the food in the halogen oven, fit and close the lid, set the timer and temperature dials, and away you go …

Some recipes do require particular cooking techniques that involve the use of the hob, but these are generally uncomplicated and are designed so that you achieve the best possible flavours and textures in the finished dish, while still making the most of your halogen oven. You will still be saving time and energy – and putting great food on the table!

vegetables

It is essential to remember that vegetables will generally take longer to cook than any meat, so you will need to start cooking them first, particularly vegetables such as carrots and potatoes. You can cook them directly on the

racks or even in a casserole dish with a little water or oil?

general advice

1 The glass lid gets very hot, as do other oven surfaces, so avoid touching the lid without wearing oven gloves.

2 Always check whether the meat is fully cooked before serving. The ovens have a tendency to brown meat quite quickly on the outside.

3 Use foil to avoid burning food, and remove for the last 5 minutes of cooking time.

4 Keep the halogen oven clean (see page 12) and clean the lid with a damp cloth regularly.

about these recipes

All the recipes have been designed for use with a halogen oven and require the basic skill level of someone who is used to working in a kitchen. The majority of the recipes also provide variations on the main recipe either by slightly altering the ingredients and sometimes the techniques used, or by providing an additional element to the dish, such as a sauce or vegetable accompaniment. It is advisable that you familiarize yourself with your halogen oven before using it for the first time and that, when it comes to particular recipes, you ensure that you have any additional equipment needed on hand. Read the instructions thoroughly and make sure that work surfaces are clear and, before using the oven, make sure that it is clean, securely positioned and free from any obstructions, and that the power cord is not touching anything hot (or soon-to-be hot!).

chicken

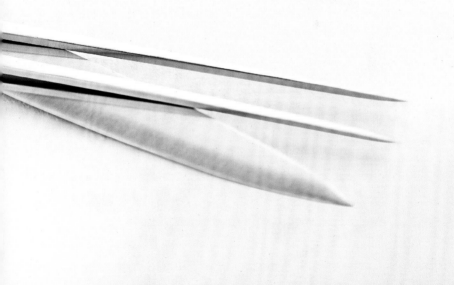

grape & yogurt honey chicken

Serves **4**

Preparation time **10 minutes**

Cooking time **about 1 hour 10 minutes**

3 tablespoons **clear honey**

2 teaspoons **dry mustard powder**

2 teaspoons **dark soy sauce**

1.5 kg (3 lb) **oven-ready chicken**

150 ml (¼ pint) **chicken stock**

150 ml (¼ pint) **dry white wine**

125 g (4 oz) **seedless green grapes**, halved

150 ml (¼ pint) **low-fat natural yogurt**, at room temperature

salt and **pepper**

Mix together the honey, 1 teaspoon salt, mustard and soy sauce in a small bowl. Place the chicken on the lower rack of the halogen oven and spread the honey mixture over it. Pour the stock into the bowl of the oven.

Set the temperature to 200°C (392°F) and cook the chicken for 1 hour, turning it after 20 minutes' cooking time, then back again after another 20 minutes. Check that the meat is cooked through by piercing the thickest area of the thigh with a knife; the juices should run clear. Cook for a little longer if needed. Leave the chicken to rest in a warm place while you finish preparing the sauce.

Add the wine to the bowl with the stock. Increase the temperature to 250°C (482°F) and cook for 6–8 minutes until the juices are bubbling. Stir in the grapes and cook for a further 2 minutes until hot.

Pour the sauce into a warm serving jug and stir in the yogurt. Season to taste with salt and pepper, and spoon a little over the chicken. Serve the chicken with the remaining sauce, buttered new potatoes and mangetout or sugarsnap peas.

For gingered chicken with lime & coconut, mix the glaze as above, using a 15 g (½ oz) piece of fresh root ginger, grated, the grated rind of 2 limes and 1 tablespoon lime juice instead of the mustard and soy sauce. For the sauce, use an additional 150 ml (¼ pint) chicken stock and 25 g (1 oz) grated creamed coconut instead of the wine. Omit the grapes and sprinkle the cooked chicken with chopped coriander.

simple chicken curry

Serves **4**
Preparation time **15 minutes**
Cooking time **35 minutes**

2 tablespoons **sunflower oil**
500 g (1 lb) diced **boneless,
  skinless chicken thighs**
2 **onions**, thinly sliced
2 **garlic cloves**, crushed
1 tablespoon **medium curry
  paste**
2 tablespoons **tomato purée**
75 g (3 oz) **creamed coconut**,
  grated
2 **bay leaves**
1 tablespoon **lemon juice**
450 ml (¾ pint) **chicken** or
  vegetable stock
300 g (10 oz) **potatoes**, diced
salt
coriander leaves to garnish

Heat the oil in a frying pan on the hob and gently fry the chicken, stirring, until pale golden. Stir in the onions and fry for a further 5 minutes. Add the garlic and curry paste and fry for a further 1 minute.

Stir in the remaining ingredients, season with salt and bring just to the boil. Transfer to a casserole dish and cover with foil. Place the casserole dish on the lower rack of the halogen oven.

Set the temperature to 200°C (392°F) and cook for 25 minutes or until the chicken is cooked through. Garnish with coriander leaves and serve with warm naan bread or chapattis and wilted spinach.

For Keralan chicken curry, crush 12 cardamom pods using a mortar and pestle. Remove the husks and crush the seeds a little more. Make the curry as above, replacing the curry paste, tomato purée, bay leaves and lemon juice with the crushed cardamom, ½ cinnamon stick, several crushed dried curry leaves, ½ teaspoon ground turmeric, 1 finely chopped fresh green chilli and 4 skinned, deseeded and diced tomatoes.

chicken & chorizo burgers

Serves **4**

Preparation time **15 minutes,
  plus chilling**

Cooking time **12 minutes**

200 g (7 oz) **natural cottage
  cheese**

50 g (2 oz) **cooking chorizo
  sausage**, skinned and diced

½ **onion**, roughly chopped

225 g (7½ oz) **minced
  chicken**

1 tbsp chopped **oregano**

vegetable oil for oiling

salt and **pepper**

To serve

4 **burger buns**

leafy green salad

spicy relish

Put the cottage cheese in a sieve over a large bowl and press the mixture through the sieve with the back of a spoon. Set aside.

Process the chorizo and onion in a food processor until finely chopped. Add the chicken and oregano, season with salt and pepper and process until mixed. Tip into the cheese and mix well until evenly combined. (This is best done with your hands.)

Divide the mixture into 4 even-sized pieces and shape each one into a burger. Chill for at least 1 hour.

Place the burgers in a lightly oiled shallow roasting tin on the upper rack of the halogen oven. Set the temperature to 200°C (392°F) and cook the burgers for 12 minutes, turning them once, until cooked through. Serve in burger buns with a leafy green salad and spicy relish.

For Gruyère, pork & bacon burgers, finely chop 75 g (3 oz) smoked back bacon and mix with 1 small finely chopped onion, 400 g (13 oz) lean minced pork, 3 tablespoons chopped parsley and plenty of pepper. Shape into burgers and cook in the halogen oven as above. Once cooked, top the burgers with 75 g (3 oz) grated Gruyère cheese and cook briefly until the cheese melts. Serve in Granary buns.

five-spice chicken

Serves **4**

Preparation time **10 minutes, plus marinating**

Cooking time **25 minutes**

4 medium **boneless, skinless chicken breasts**, about 200 g (7 oz) each, cut into 2.5 cm (1 inch) chunks

2 **shallots**, thinly sliced

1 **garlic clove**, crushed

2 tablespoons **light soy sauce**

1 tablespoon **dry sherry**

½ teaspoon **five-spice powder**

To garnish

1 **spring onion**, finely chopped

sesame seeds

chopped **coriander**

Mix the chicken in a bowl with the shallots, garlic, soy sauce, sherry and five-spice powder. Cover loosely and leave to marinate in the refrigerator for at least 1 hour or overnight.

Place a sheet of foil over the upper rack of the halogen oven, turning the edges up so that the juices will be contained as the chicken cooks. Tip in the chicken and its marinade and spread in an even layer.

Set the temperature to 200°C (392°F) and cook for about 25 minutes, turning the chicken pieces occasionally so that they cook evenly. Serve sprinkled with the spring onion, sesame seeds and coriander, and accompany with steamed rice.

For Jamaican spiced chicken, mix the chicken in a bowl with 1 small thinly sliced red onion, 1 crushed garlic clove, 1 deseeded and finely chopped fresh red chilli, 2 teaspoons chopped thyme, 1 teaspoon ground ginger, 1 teaspoon ground coriander, 1 teaspoon ground cumin, ¼ teaspoon ground turmeric and 2 tablespoons vegetable oil. Cover and chill as above. Cook on the foil-lined rack as above, adding 50 g (2 oz) roughly chopped raw cashew nuts for the last minute of cooking.

chicken goujons with oven chips

Serves **4**
Preparation time **25 minutes**
Cooking time **50 minutes**

75 g (3 oz) **dried
breadcrumbs**
3 tablespoons grated
Parmesan cheese
1 tablespoon chopped
oregano or **parsley**
1 **egg**
4 medium **boneless, skinless
chicken breasts**, about
200 g (7 oz) each, cut into
1 cm (½ inch) strips
500 g (1 lb) **potatoes**
1 tablespoon **sunflower oil**,
plus extra for oiling
salt and **pepper**

Tartare sauce
150 ml (¼ pint) **mayonnaise**
40 g (1½ oz) **gherkins**, finely
chopped
1 **garlic clove**, crushed
1 tablespoon **capers**, rinsed,
drained and finely chopped
2 tablespoons chopped
chives

Cut the potatoes into chunky chips and toss in a bowl with the oil and plenty of salt and pepper. Scatter in a lightly oiled shallow roasting tin and place on the lower rack of the halogen oven. Set the temperature to 200°C (392°F) and cook for 20 minutes, turning once.

Meanwhile mix together the breadcrumbs, Parmesan, oregano or parsley and a little salt and pepper. Tip out on to a plate. Beat the egg on a separate plate.

Coat the chicken strips in the egg, then the bread-crumbs, and space them slightly apart in an oiled shallow roasting tin. Place on the upper rack of the halogen oven. Leaving the chips on the bottom rack, cook them with the chicken for a further 30 minutes, turning the chicken goujons once, until chicken and chips are golden brown.

Make the tartare sauce. Mix together the mayonnaise, gherkins, garlic, capers and chives, and season with a little salt and pepper. Turn into a small serving bowl. Serve the goujons and chips piping hot, accompanied by the tartare sauce, lemon wedges and a leafy salad.

For aïoli to serve instead of the tartare sauce, crush 1 plump garlic clove and put in a food processor with 2 egg yolks. Blend briefly to combine. With the machine running, gradually pour in 200 ml (7 fl oz) mild olive oil in a thin, steady stream until thickened. Blend in 1 tablespoon white wine vinegar and salt and pepper to taste. (If the aïoli separates while adding the oil, tip it into a measuring jug and add another egg yolk to the bowl of the food processor. Gradually add the separated mixture to the machine to make a smooth sauce.)

baked chicken with indian spices

Serves **4**

Preparation time **10 minutes**

Cooking time **45 minutes**

75 g (3 oz) **butter**

3 large **onions**, thinly sliced

2 teaspoons **ground turmeric**

3 cm (1¼ inch) piece of **fresh root ginger**, finely chopped

6 **whole cloves**

1 **cinnamon stick**, halved

3 **garlic cloves**, thinly sliced

1.25 kg (2½ lb) **oven-ready chicken**, jointed into 10 pieces

salt and **pepper**

Melt 50 g (2 oz) of the butter in a frying pan on the hob and gently fry the onions for 8–10 minutes until softened and beginning to colour.

Drain the onions from the pan using a slotted spoon and put in a casserole dish. Melt the remaining butter in the pan and add the turmeric, ginger, cloves, cinnamon and garlic. Add the chicken pieces and turn in the spices over a gentle heat for 5 minutes.

Mix the chicken and their spices with the onions in the casserole dish. Seaon with salt and pepper. Cover with foil and place on the lower rack of the halogen oven.

Set the temperature to 200°C (392°F) and cook for 30 minutes or until the chicken is cooked through. Serve with pilau rice, naan bread and mango chutney.

For spicy pilau rice to serve as an accompaniment, heat 2 tablespoons vegetable oil in a frying pan on the hob. Add 4 tablespoons flaked almonds and fry gently until they begin to brown. Drain the almonds with a slotted spoon and set aside. Add 1 small finely chopped onion to the pan and fry gently for 5 minutes until softened. Stir in 1 crushed garlic clove, 1 teaspoon crushed dried chillies and ½ teaspoon ground turmeric. Fry for a further 1 minute. Add 250 g (8 oz) basmati rice and 300 ml (½ pint) chicken or vegetable stock. Bring to the boil, then reduce the heat to its lowest setting. Cook gently, covered, for about 20 minutes until the rice is tender, adding a little more stock or water if the mixture becomes dry before the rice is cooked. Stir in the almonds and a handful of raisins. Season to taste with salt and pepper, and serve hot.

chicken with spicy lentils

Serves **4**
Preparation time **20 minutes**
Cooking time **50 minutes**

8 large **boneless, skinless chicken thighs**, about 100 g (3½ oz) each, cut into quarters
1 teaspoon **cumin seeds**
1 teaspoon **coriander seeds**
3 tablespoons **olive oil**
2 **garlic cloves**, crushed
2 large **red onions**, thinly sliced
100 g (3½ oz) **green lentils**, rinsed and picked over
400 g (13 oz) can **chopped tomatoes**
2 tablespoons **sun-dried tomato paste**
1 tablespoon **light muscovado sugar**
300 ml (½ pint) **chicken stock**
salt and **pepper**

Season the chicken pieces with salt and pepper. Crush the cumin and coriander seeds using a mortar and pestle.

Heat the oil in a frying pan on the hob and gently fry the chicken for 5 minutes, stirring, until beginning to colour. Stir in the garlic, onions and crushed spices. Fry gently for a further 3 minutes, stirring.

Turn into a casserole dish and add the lentils. Bring the tomatoes, tomato paste, sugar and chicken stock to the boil in the frying pan and pour over the chicken and lentils. Mix the ingredients to combine and season with salt and pepper. Cover the dish with foil and place on the lower rack of the halogen oven.

Set the temperature to 200°C (392°F) and cook for about 40 minutes until the chicken is cooked through. Serve the dish with warm flat breads and a roasted tomato salad.

For Moroccan chicken with chickpeas, fry the chicken as above, then add the garlic and onions, and replace the cumin and coriander seeds with 2 teaspoons ras el hanout spice blend. Turn into the casserole dish and add the tomatoes, tomato paste, sugar and stock. Replace the lentils with a 400 g (13 oz) can chickpeas, drained. Cook as above, adding 1 tablespoon chopped mint and 50 g (2 oz) raisins for the final 5 minutes of cooking time.

chicken & mushroom casserole

Serves **4**
Preparation time **15 minutes**
Cooking time **45 minutes**

2 teaspoons **plain flour**
8 large **boneless, skinless chicken thighs,** halved
25 g (1 oz) **butter**
1 **onion**, chopped
300 ml (½ pint) **chicken stock**
several **rosemary sprigs**
200 g (7 oz) **chestnut mushrooms**, sliced
4 tablespoons **crème fraîche**
salt and **pepper**

Season the flour with salt and pepper. Toss the chicken pieces in the flour.

Melt the butter in a frying pan on the hob and fry the chicken pieces and onion for 5 minutes or until beginning to brown. Pour in the stock, stir through and bring to the boil. Transfer to a casserole dish and add the rosemary, mushrooms and a little salt and pepper. Cover with foil and place on the lower rack of the halogen oven.

Set the temperature to 200°C (392°F) and cook for 40 minutes, removing the foil for the last 5 minutes of cooking time. Remove from the oven and stir in the crème fraîche. Check the seasoning and serve with celeriac and potato mash and seasonal vegetables.

For celeriac and potato mash to serve as an accompaniment, cut 300 g (10 oz) celeriac and 300 g (10 oz) floury potatoes into small chunks and cook in salted boiling water for about 20 minutes until tender. Drain and return to the saucepan. Add 100 ml (3½ fl oz) crème fraiche, 25 g (1 oz) butter and 1 tablespoon Dijon mustard. Mash until completely smooth, adding a little salt to taste if needed.

sticky glazed chicken drumsticks

Serves **4**
Preparation time **10 minutes,
plus marinating**
Cooking time **25 minutes**

4 tablespoons **red wine
vinegar**
2 tablespoons **dark soy sauce**
2 tablespoons **tomato purée**
2 **garlic cloves**, crushed
generous pinch of **cayenne
pepper**
1 tablespoon **Worcestershire
sauce**
2 tablespoons **clear honey**
8 large **chicken drumsticks**,
skinned
vegetable oil for brushing

Mix together the vinegar, soy sauce, tomato purée, garlic, cayenne pepper, Worcestershire sauce and honey in a small bowl.

Make 2 or 3 deep slits in the fleshy side of each drumstick. Place in a shallow glass or ceramic dish and add the marinade, turning the chicken drumsticks until coated. Cover loosely with clingfilm and leave to marinate in the refrigerator for at least 2 hours, or overnight.

Place a sheet of foil over the upper rack of the halogen oven, turning up the edges so that the juices will be contained as the chicken cooks. Brush lightly with oil. Arrange the chicken on the foil and spoon over the marinade.

Set the temperature to 200°C (392°F) and cook for 25 minutes, turning the chicken occasionally and brushing with the marinade, until cooked through. Serve with buttered corn on the cob and a watercress salad.

For herb-crusted chicken drumsticks, mix together 50 g (2 oz) dried breadcrumbs with 50 g (2 oz) finely grated extra-mature Cheddar cheese, 2 tablespoons chopped chives and 1 tablespoon chopped tarragon. Season 2 tablespoons plain flour with salt and pepper, and use to dust the chicken. Beat 1 egg on a plate. Roll the drumsticks in the egg, then the breadcrumb mixture until evenly coated. Place on a lightly oiled piece of foil as above and drizzle with a little vegetable oil. Set the temperature to 200°C (392°F) and cook for 20–25 minutes, turning the drumsticks several times during cooking.

paprika chicken

Serves **4**

Preparation time **20 minutes**

Cooking time **1 hour**, plus resting

2 **red onions**, cut into wedges

6 **garlic cloves**, unpeeled

2 teaspoons **paprika**

2 tablespoons **olive oil**

1.5 kg (3 lb) **oven-ready chicken**

a few **rosemary sprigs**

2 **red peppers**, cored, deseeded and cut into strips

2 **yellow** or **orange peppers**, cored, deseeded and cut into strips

200 g (7 oz) **cooking chorizo sausage**, skinned and diced

4 small **tomatoes**, halved

salt and **pepper**

Put the onion wedges and garlic in a roasting tin. Stir in 1 teaspoon of the paprika and 1 tablespoon of the oil. Place the chicken on top, breast-side face down.

Push the rosemary sprigs into the chicken cavity and place the tin on the lower rack of the halogen oven.

Set the temperature to 200°C (392°F) and roast the chicken for 30 minutes. Transfer the chicken to a plate and add the peppers, chorizo and tomatoes to the roasting tin. Place the chicken on top of the vegetables, breast-side face up. Brush with the remaining oil, sprinkle with the remaining paprika and season with salt and pepper. Cook for a further 25–30 minutes until the chicken is cooked through – check by piercing the thickest area of the thigh with a knife; the juices should run clear. If needed, cook for a little longer.

Leave the chicken to rest in a warm place for 15 minutes before carving. Serve with the vegetables and chorizo, saffron rice and a tomato salad.

For saffron rice to serve as an accompaniment, gently toast 40 g (1½ oz) pine nuts in a dry frying pan until golden; remove and set aside. Next, fry 1 chopped onion in 3 tablespoons olive oil for 5 minutes, adding 1 peeled garlic clove for the final minute. Stir in 225 g (7½ oz) long-grain rice and pour over 300 ml (½ pint) chicken or vegetable stock. Crumble in ½ teaspoon saffron threads. Bring to a simmer, cover with a lid and cook gently for 15 minutes until the rice is just tender, adding a dash of water if the mixture dries out. Add the pine nuts to the pan, season to taste with salt and pepper and stir in 4 tablespoons chopped coriander to serve.

beef

chilli pepper burgers

Serves **4**

Preparation time **15 minutes, plus chilling**

Cooking time **12 minutes**

450 g (14½ oz) **lean minced beef**

1 small **onion**, finely chopped

1 **garlic clove**, crushed

1 small **red pepper**, cored, deseeded and finely diced

½ teaspoon **dried mixed herbs**

2 tablespoons **sweet chilli sauce**

40g (1½ oz) **fresh white breadcrumbs**

1 **egg**, beaten

1 tablespoon **sunflower** or **vegetable oil**

salt and **pepper**

To serve

4 **burger buns**

handful of **crisp lettuce leaves**

tomato slices

red onion slices

Put the mince in a bowl and add the onion, garlic, red pepper, herbs, sweet chilli sauce and breadcrumbs. Add the egg and season with a little salt and pepper. Mix well. (This is best done with your hands.) Shape the mixture into 4 large burgers, and place on a baking sheet lined with nonstick baking paper. Cover loosely and chill for at least 30 minutes.

Brush each burger lightly with the oil and place on the upper rack of the halogen oven.

Set the temperature to 200°C (392°F) and grill for about 12 minutes, turning halfway through cooking, until cooked through. Serve in the burger buns with crisp lettuce leaves and tomato and onion slices, and accompany with mayonnaise and relish or pickle.

For coriander & cucumber pickle to serve as an accompaniment, put 2 teaspoons mustard seeds in a small frying pan and heat until the seeds start to pop. Remove from the heat and tip into a bowl so that they don't overcook. Process 150 g (5 oz) roughly chopped dill pickled cucumber and 1 roughly chopped shallot in a food processor until chopped into small pieces. Add 5 g (¼ oz) roughly chopped coriander and process until finely chopped. Tip into a bowl and stir in the toasted mustard seeds, 2 tablespoons pickling juice from the jar and 1 tablespoon caster sugar. Stir well to mix and store in the refrigerator for up to 3 days.

steak & kidney pies

Serves **4**

Preparation time **40 minutes, plus cooling**

Cooking time about **1 hour 40 minutes**

2 tablespoons **vegetable oil**

450 g (14½ oz) **lean braising steak**, cut into small pieces

225 g (7½ oz) **ox kidney**, cored, trimmed and cut into small chunks

1 **onion**, thinly sliced

100 g (3½ oz) **chestnut mushrooms**, quartered

2 tablespoons **plain flour**, plus extra for dusting

450 ml (¾ pint) hot **beef stock**

150 ml (¼ pint) **ale**

400 g (13 oz) **ready-made shortcrust pastry**

beaten **egg**, for glazing

salt and **pepper**

Heat 1 tablespoon of the oil in a large frying pan on the hob and fry the beef, in batches, until browned on all sides, draining each batch to a plate. Add the kidney to the pan and fry for a further 5 minutes; drain. Add the remaining oil, onion and mushrooms to the pan and fry gently for a further 5 minutes.

Return all the ingredients to the pan, including any juices from the beef, and sprinkle in the flour, stirring for 1 minute. Add the stock and ale, and bring to the boil. Season with salt and pepper, and transfer to a casserole dish. Cover with foil and place on the lower rack of the halogen oven.

Set the temperature to 200°C (392°F) and cook for about 50 minutes until the meat is tender. Check the seasoning and leave to cool.

Transfer the mixture to 4 individual pie dishes or one large dish, on the lower rack of the halogen oven. Do not fill each dish with liquid to more than 1.5 cm (¾ inch) from the top. Serve any excess in a jug.

Roll the pastry out on a lightly floured surface and cut out a lid or lids that are about 1 cm (½ inch) larger than stacking the dishes or dish. Position the pastry, crimping it around the edges to seal. Brush the pastry with beaten egg to glaze, sprinkle with a little salt and place on the lower rack of the halogen oven.

Set the temperature to 225°C (437°F) and cook for 25–30 minutes, covering the pastry with foil if it starts to brown too much. (If using one large dish, increase the cooking time to 35 minutes.) Serve with minted peas and sautéed potatoes.

asian ginger beef

Serves **6**
Preparation time **25 minutes**
Cooking time **1 hour 10
   minutes**

3 tablespoons **wok** or
   stir-fry oil
700 g (1 lb 6 oz) **lean braising
   steak**, cut into small chunks
2 **celery sticks**, sliced
2 **red peppers**, cored,
   deseeded and cut into
   chunks
400 ml (14 fl oz) hot **beef**
   or **vegetable stock**
1 tablespoon **dark soy sauce**
3 cm (1¼ inch) piece of **fresh
   root ginger**, grated
½ teaspoon crushed **dried red
   chillies**
1 tablespoon **cornflour**
2 tablespoons **water**
200 g (7 oz) **sugarsnap peas**,
   halved lengthways
½ bunch of **spring onions**,
   sliced

Heat 2 tablespoons of the oil in a large frying pan
on the hob and fry the beef, in batches, until lightly
browned. Transfer to a casserole dish. Add the
remaining oil to the pan and fry the celery and
peppers until beginning to soften. Add to the dish.

Pour over the stock and add the soy sauce, ginger and
chillies. Stir gently to mix. Cover with foil and place on
the lower rack of the halogen oven.

Set the temperature to 200°C (392°F) and cook for
50 minutes or until the beef is tender. Blend the
cornflour with the water. Stir into the beef and add the
sugarsnap peas and spring onions. Cover and cook for
a further 10 minutes. Serve with Thai fragrant rice.

For chilli beef with pumpkin, cut 500 g (1 lb)
pumpkin or butternut squash into small dice, discarding
the skin and seeds. Fry the beef and vegetables as
above, using 3 tablespoons light vegetable oil such as
groundnut, rapeseed or coconut oil instead of infused
wok or stir-fry oil. Replace the soy sauce and chillies
with 2 tablespoons tomato purée and 1 tablespoon
muscovado sugar. Finish as above, replacing the
sugarsnap peas with 200 g (7 oz) frozen peas,
and serve with fresh crusty bread.

grilled steak with sorrel sauce

Serves **4**

Preparation time **10 minutes**

Cooking time **15 minutes**

4 **fillet steaks**, about 175 g
   (6 oz) each
1 **garlic clove**, crushed
50 g (2 oz) **butter**
2 **shallots**, finely chopped
150 ml (¼ pint) **single cream**
75 g (3 oz) **sorrel**, shredded
salt and **pepper**

Rub the steaks with the garlic and a little salt and pepper. Place on the upper rack of the halogen oven. Set the temperature to 250°C (482°F) and cook for 3 minutes on each side. (Cook a little longer if you prefer your steaks well done.) Remove from the oven and leave to rest in a warm place while making the sauce.

Remove the rack from the oven and add the butter to the bowl. Cook briefly at 200°C (392°F) until melted. Add the shallots and cook for 3 minutes. Stir in the cream and sorrel, and cook for 5 minutes until heated through. Season to taste with salt and pepper, and spoon over the steaks. Serve with chunky chips.

For steak au poivre, drain 4 teaspoons green peppercorns from their brine and crush using a mortar and pestle. Mix with a little salt and use to coat both sides of the steaks. Place on the upper rack of the halogen oven and brush with a little melted butter. Cook as above and keep warm. Make the sauce as above, omitting the sorrel and adding 2 teaspoons finely chopped thyme.

beef & barley stew

Serves **4**

Preparation time **20 minutes**

Cooking time **55 minutes**

450 g (14½ oz) **lean braising
    steak**, cut into chunks

4 **carrots**, sliced

2 **leeks**, sliced

300 g (10 oz) **swede**, cut into
    small chunks

100 g (3½ oz) **pearl barley**

1 **bouquet garni**

900 ml (1½ pints) **beef stock**

salt and **pepper**

Put the steak, carrots, leeks, swede, pearl barley and
bouquet garni in a saucepan on the hob. Add the stock
and bring to a gentle simmer.

Transfer the contents of the pan to a casserole dish
and cover with foil. Place on the lower rack of the
halogen oven.

Set the temperature to 200°C (392°F) and cook for
45–50 minutes until the meat is tender. Season to taste
with salt and pepper, and serve with potato or celeriac
mash and green beans.

For homemade beef stock, put 750 g (1½ lb) raw
beef bones in a roasting tin and cook in a preheated
oven, 200°C (400°F), Gas Mark 6, for 30 minutes
until browned. Transfer the bones to the halogen oven
and add 1 large unpeeled and halved onion, 3 sliced
carrots, 2 sliced celery sticks, several bay leaves and a
few thyme sprigs. Pour over just enough boiling water
to cover. Set the temperature to 200°C (392°F) and
cook for 15 minutes. Reduce the temperature to 160°C
(320°F) and cook for a further 1½ hours. Strain and
leave to cool. Store in the refrigerator for up to a week
or freeze for up to 4 months until needed.

roast sirloin of beef

Serves **4–5**
Preparation time **15 minutes**
Cooking time **50 minutes,**
  plus resting

1.25 kg (2½ lb) **rolled sirloin**
  of beef
2 large **onions**, sliced
several **thyme sprigs**
2 tablespoons **olive oil**
2 teaspoons **plain flour**
2 teaspoons **dry mustard**
  powder
200 ml (7 fl oz) **red wine**
salt and **pepper**

Rub the beef on all sides with plenty of salt and pepper. Scatter the onions and thyme sprigs in the bottom of a roasting tin and rest the beef on top. Drizzle with the oil.

Set the temperature to 225°C (437°F) and cook for 20 minutes, turning twice during cooking. Mix together the flour and mustard powder. Turn the meat so that the fat side is uppermost and sprinkle with the flour mixture. Cook for a further 15 minutes. (The beef will still be pink in the centre, so cook for a little longer if you prefer beef cooked through.) Transfer the meat to a board or platter, and leave to rest for 20 minutes before carving and while making the gravy.

Skim any fat from the juices in the tin, return to the halogen oven and fry the onions for 10 minutes. Pour in the wine and cook for a further 5 minutes. Season to taste with salt and pepper, and strain into a gravy jug. Serve hot with the beef and baby carrots or vegetables of your choice.

For beef with beetroot & horseradish, put 6 small uncooked and unpeeled beetroot in a saucepan on the hob and cover with water. Bring to the boil and cook for 20 minutes until softened. Drain, peel away the skins and quarter the beetroot. Cut 2 large red onions into wedges. Cook the beef with the thyme as above, scattering the red onions around the meat instead of the sliced onions and adding the beetroot. Remove the beetroot and onions from the oven with the meat and add 1 tablespoon hot horseradish sauce when making the gravy.

beef stroganoff

Serves **4**

Preparation time **15 minutes**

Cooking time **45 minutes**

25 g (1 oz) **butter**

625 g (1¼ lb) **lean rump steak**, trimmed and cut into 1 cm (½ inch) strips

2 **onions**, thinly sliced

200 g (7 oz) **button mushrooms**, halved

400 g (13 oz) **can cream of mushroom soup**

2 tablespoons **Worcestershire sauce**

4 tablespoons **crème fraîche**

salt and **pepper**

finely chopped parsley to garnish

Put the butter in the bowl of the halogen oven and heat briefly at 250°C (482°F) until melted. Season the beef with salt and pepper, and add to the oven with the onions. Cook for 10 minutes.

Stir in the mushrooms, mushroom soup, Worcestershire sauce and a little seasoning. Reduce the heat to 200°C (392°F) and cook for 30 minutes. Stir in the crème fraîche and check the seasoning. Garnish with finely chopped parsley and serve with mixed wild and white rice.

For beef & tomato goulash, cook the beef with the onions as above, adding 2 crushed garlic cloves and 1 tablespoon hot paprika once the onions have softened slightly. Stir in a 400 g (13 oz) can cream of tomato soup, 1 teaspoon caraway seeds and 4 deseeded and chopped tomatoes. Cook for 30 minutes until the beef is tender. Spoon over boiled rice and serve topped with spoonfuls of soured cream.

aubergine thai green curry

Serves **4**

Preparation time **15 minutes**

Cooking time **40 minutes**

3 tablespoons **vegetable oil**

1 small **aubergine**, diced

3 tablespoons **Thai green
curry paste**

400 ml (14 fl oz) **coconut milk**

150 ml (¼ pint) **beef** or
chicken stock

450 g (14½ oz) **rump** or
sirloin steak, cut into cubes

4 **kaffir lime leaves**, torn into
pieces (or a small sprinkling
of dried lime leaves)

2 tablespoons **Thai fish sauce**

2 teaspoons **palm** or **light
muscovado sugar**

shredded Thai basil leaves,
to garnish

Heat the oil in a frying pan on the hob and add the aubergine. Fry gently for 5 minutes until the aubergine starts to colour, then stir in the curry paste. Fry gently for a further 2 minutes, then mix in the coconut milk and stock. Cook gently for 5 minutes.

Stir in the beef, kaffir lime leaves, fish sauce and sugar. Transfer to a casserole dish, cover with foil and place on the lower rack of the halogen oven.

Set the temperature to 200°C (392°F) and cook for 25 minutes or until the meat is tender. Garnish with shredded Thai basil leaves and serve with rice.

For aromatic rice to serve as an accompaniment, cook 375 g (12 oz) Thai fragrant rice in lightly salted boiling water until tender. Drain and return to the saucepan. Grate 25 g (1 oz) creamed coconut into the pan and stir into the hot rice. Add 2 finely chopped spring onions, the finely grated rind of 2 limes and 15 g (½ oz) finely chopped coriander. Season to taste with salt and pepper. Serve hot.

chilli-spiced meatballs

Serves **4**
Preparation time **25 minutes**
Cooking time **20 minutes**

1 large **onion**, roughly
  chopped
1 **fresh red chilli**, deseeded
  and chopped
2 **garlic cloves**, chopped
1 teaspoon **shrimp paste**
2 teaspoons **coriander seeds**
2 teaspoons **cumin seeds**
450 g (14½ oz) **lean minced
  beef**
2 teaspoons **dark soy sauce**
1 teaspoon **dark muscovado
  sugar**
juice of ½ **lemon**
1 **egg**, beaten
vegetable oil, for oiling
salt and **pepper**
finely sliced **spring onions**
  to garnish

Put the onion, chilli, garlic and shrimp paste in a food processor and process to a paste, or grind to a paste using a mortar and pestle. (Don't overmix or the onion will become too wet.)

Heat the coriander and cumin seeds in a small frying pan on the hob until they start to release their aroma. Grind in a pestle and mortar. Put the minced beef in a mixing bowl and add the onion mixture, toasted coriander and cumin seeds, soy sauce, sugar and lemon juice. Add the beaten egg and mix until evenly combined. (This is best done with your hands.)

Shape the mixture into balls, each about the size of a golf ball. Lightly oil a shallow roasting tin or ovenproof dish and add the meatballs. Place on the upper rack of the halogen oven.

Set the temperature to 200°C (392°F) and grill the meatballs for 15–20 minutes until cooked through. Serve with noodles and a sweet dipping sauce, garnished with finely sliced spring onions.

For Stilton-stuffed meatballs, cut 100 g (3½ oz) Stilton cheese into 1 cm (½ inch) cubes. In a food processor, process 1 red onion and 1 garlic clove until chopped. Add the lean minced beef, 2 tablespoons chopped parsley, 1 tablespoon chopped thyme and a little salt and pepper. Divide the mixture into 24 pieces and roll each into balls, pressing a piece of the cheese into the centre of each one. Cook the meatballs as above and serve with buttered linguine and cranberry relish or sauce.

beef & ale stew

Serves **4**

Preparation time **20 minutes**

Cooking time **1 hour**

2 tablespoons **plain flour**

500 g (1 lb) **lean braising steak**, cut into small chunks

40 g (1½ oz) **butter**

1 tablespoon **vegetable oil**

1 **onion**, chopped

2 **carrots**, sliced lengthways and roughly chopped

2 **celery sticks**, roughly chopped

450 ml (¾ pint) **ale**

150 ml (¼ pint) **beef stock**

2 tablespoons **tomato purée**

1 tablespoon **muscovado sugar**

2 teaspoons **wholegrain mustard**

salt and **pepper**

Season the flour with salt and pepper, and use to coat the beef. Melt the butter with the oil in a large frying pan on the hob. Fry the beef, in batches, until browned. Transfer to a casserole dish. Add the onion, carrots and celery to the frying pan and fry gently for a further 5 minutes. Add to the casserole dish.

Pour the ale and stock into the frying pan and add the tomato purée, sugar, mustard and a little salt and pepper. Bring just to the boil and pour into the casserole dish. Cover with foil and place on the lower rack of the halogen oven.

Set the temperature to 200°C (392°F) and cook for about 50 minutes until the meat is tender. Check the seasoning before serving. Serve with a root mash.

For herb & parsnip mash to serve as an accompaniment cook 1.5 kg (3 lb) small parsnips in plenty of lightly salted boiling water until tender. Drain and return to the pan. Mash until broken up, then add 100 ml (3½ fl oz) milk, 50 g (2 oz) butter, 2 finely chopped spring onions, 2 tablespoons finely chopped parsley, 1 tablespoon chopped lemon thyme and salt and pepper to taste. Mash well until smooth.

spanish burgers & mayonnaise

Serves **4**

Preparation time **20 minutes,
    plus soaking**

Cooking time **16 minutes**

1 small **white bread roll**

2 **garlic cloves**, crushed

100 ml (3½ fl oz) **mayonnaise**

1 **onion**, roughly chopped

450 g (14½ oz) **lean minced
    beef**

1 **egg**, beaten

1 tablespoon chopped
    oregano

10 **pimiento-stuffed green
    olives**, roughly chopped

olive oil, for brushing

1 **beefsteak tomato**

4 **canned anchovy fillets**,
    drained and halved
    lengthways

salt and **pepper**

Tear up the bread roll and put in a bowl. Cover with cold water and leave to soften for 15 minutes.

Beat one of the garlic cloves and a little salt and pepper into the mayonnaise and transfer to a small serving dish. Set aside.

Squeeze all the water out of the bread and put the bread in a food processor with the onion, remaining garlic, minced beef, egg and oregano. Season with salt and pepper, and process briefly to mix. Add the olives and process until they are chopped into the mixture. Shape into 4 even-sized burgers and place on the upper rack of the halogen oven. Brush with oil.

Set the temperature to 200°C (392°F) and grill the burgers for 15 minutes, turning once halfway through cooking, until cooked through.

Cut 4 slices, each about 1 cm (½ inch) thick, from the tomato and place a slice over each burger. Arrange the anchovies on top and cook for a further 1 minute. Serve with the garlic mayonnaise and a leafy salad.

For chilli burgers with tomato salsa, make the burgers as above, replacing the olives with 1 deseeded and finely chopped fresh red chilli. Cook as above, omitting the tomato and anchovy topping. For the salsa, halve and scoop the pulp from 200 g (7 oz) vine-ripened tomatoes. Press through a sieve over a bowl, removing the juice; reserve. Finely chop the tomato and mix with 2 finely chopped spring onions, a handful of chopped coriander, 2 teaspoons caster sugar, 2 teaspoons lemon juice, the reserved tomato juice and a little salt and pepper. Serve with the burgers.

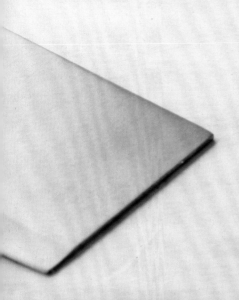

pork

chilli pork ribs

Serves **4–6**

Preparation time **10 minutes, plus marinating**

Cooking time **20 minutes**

100 ml (3½ fl oz) **sunflower oil**

2 teaspoons **chilli powder**

1 teaspoon **barbecue seasoning**

finely grated rind and juice of **1 lime**

2 **garlic cloves**, crushed

3 tablespoons **tomato ketchup**

16–18 **pork spare ribs**

Mix together the oil, chilli powder, barbecue seasoning, lime rind and juice, garlic and tomato ketchup in a small bowl.

Put the ribs in a shallow glass or ceramic dish and brush with the marinade. Cover loosely and leave to marinate in the refrigerator for at least 2 hours.

Arrange the ribs on the upper rack of the halogen oven. Set the temperature to 200°C (392°F) and cook the ribs for about 20 minutes, turning them once, until golden. Serve with jacket potatoes and a salad.

For sausages with sweet potatoes, cook 350 g (11½ oz) diced sweet potatoes in boiling water for 5 minutes until softened. Drain well. Arrange 8 good-quality pork sausages in a shallow ovenproof dish and drizzle with 2 tablespoons olive oil. Scatter with 1 thinly sliced large red onion and place on the upper rack of the halogen oven. Set the temperature to 200°C (392°F) and cook for 10 minutes. Add the potatoes and stir to mix. Drizzle with another 1 tablespoon olive oil and 1 tablespoon clear honey. Cook for a further 15–20 minutes, turning once or twice, until the sausages are golden. Serve drizzled with 2 tablespoons balsamic vinegar and scattered with chopped parsley.

caribbean pork with pineapple

Serves **2**

Preparation time **15 minutes**

Cooking time **40 minutes**

1 tablespoon **vegetable oil**

250 g (8 oz) **pork tenderloin**, cubed

1 small **onion**, chopped

100 g (3½ oz) **chestnut mushrooms**, sliced

1 teaspoon chopped **thyme**

¼ teaspoon **cayenne pepper**

150 ml (¼ pint) **chicken stock**

225 g (7½ oz) **can pineapple slices in natural juice**, drained and cut into chunks (reserve the juice)

1 tablespoon **cornflour**

2 tablespoons **water**

salt

Heat the oil in a frying pan on the hob and lightly fry the pork and onion for 5 minutes until beginning to brown. Transfer to a casserole dish. Add the mushrooms to the pan and fry for 5 minutes, then add to the casserole.

Stir the thyme, cayenne, chicken stock and pineapple and its reserved juice into the casserole. Bring to the boil and pour over the pork. Cover the dish with foil and place on the lower rack of the halogen oven.

Set the temperature to 200°C (392°F) and cook for 25 minutes or until the pork is tender. In a small bowl, blend the cornflour with the measurement water. Using a slotted spoon, remove the pork from the casserole and stir the cornflour paste into the liquid. Season to taste with salt and return the pork to the dish. Cover and cook for a further 5 minutes. Serve hot with steamed rice.

For pork with basil & peppers, in a frying pan on the hob, fry the pork with the onion as above using 1 tablespoon olive oil and transfer to a casserole dish. Using the same pan, heat a further 1 tablespoon olive oil and fry 2 cored, deseeded and chopped red peppers. Add to the casserole. Next, add ½ x 400 g (13 oz) can chopped tomatoes to the casserole with 2 tablespoons basil pesto, 150 ml (¼ pint) chicken stock, 1 teaspoon caster sugar and salt and pepper to taste. Cook as above, stirring in a handful of torn basil leaves 5 minutes before the end of cooking time.

pork chops ardennaise

Serves **4**

Preparation time **20 minutes**

Cooking time **45 minutes**

4 **pork loin chops**, 200 g
   (7 oz) each

25 g (1 oz) **butter**

1 tablespoon **vegetable oil**

100 g (3½ oz) **button
   mushrooms**, halved

100 g (3½ oz) **diced pancetta**

12 **shallots**, peeled and left
   whole

300 ml (½ pint) **dry white
   wine**

1 tablespoon **cornflour**

2 tablespoons **water**

1 tablespoon **French mustard**

150 ml (¼ pint) **single cream**

salt and **pepper**

chopped **parsley**, to garnish

Season the pork chops with salt and pepper. Melt the butter with the oil in a frying pan on the hob and fry the chops on both sides to brown. Transfer to a casserole dish. Add the mushrooms, pancetta and shallots to the same frying pan and fry gently, stirring, for 5 minutes. Add to the casserole.

Pour the wine into the pan and bring to the boil, letting it bubble for a minute and scraping up any bits from the bottom of the pan. Tip into the casserole and cover with foil. Place on the lower rack of the halogen oven.

Set the temperature to 200°C (392°F) and cook for 30 minutes. In a small bowl, blend the cornflour with the measurement water. Remove the chops from the casserole and add the cornflour paste, mustard and cream to the liquid. Season to taste with salt and pepper, and return the pork to the dish. Cover and cook for a further 5 minutes. Serve hot, sprinkled with parsley.

For pork chops with cider & prunes, cook the pork as above, replacing the mushrooms with 1 chopped fennel bulb and the wine with 300 ml (½ pint) cider. Stir in 8 sliced sage leaves. Add the cornflour paste, mustard and cream as above, stirring in 75 g (3 oz) halved pitted prunes.

pork with dumplings

Serves **4**

Preparation time **25 minutes**

Cooking time **55 minutes**

450 g (14½ oz) **lean diced pork**

50 g (2oz) **butter**

100 g (3½ oz) **streaky bacon**, diced

3 small **leeks**, sliced

25 g (1 oz) **plain flour**

450 ml (¾ pint) **semi-skimmed milk**

1 tablespoon chopped **thyme**

2 teaspoons **mild chilli powder**

salt and **pepper**

Dumplings

75 g (3 oz) **plain flour**

75 g (3 oz) **wholemeal flour**

2 teaspoons **baking powder**

3 tablespoons **dried breadcrumbs**

2 tablespoons chopped **chives**

1 teaspoon **poppy seeds**

1 **egg**

150 ml (¼ pint) **semi-skimmed milk**

Season the pork with a little salt and pepper. Melt the butter in a frying pan on the hob and lightly brown the pork on all sides. Transfer to a casserole dish. Add the bacon and leeks to the same frying pan and fry gently for 5 minutes. Stir in the plain flour and mix to a paste. Gradually blend in the milk and whisk until smooth. Bring to the boil and stir in the thyme and chilli powder. Tip the contents of the pan into the casserole.

Cover the dish with foil and place on the lower rack of the oven. Set the temperature to 180°C (350°F) and cook for 25 minutes or until tender.

Meanwhile towards the end of the cooking time, make the dumplings. Put the 2 flours, baking powder, breadcrumbs, chives and poppy seeds in a bowl. In a separate small bowl, beat the egg with the milk and then add to the flour mixture, mixing with a round-bladed knife to form a dough and adding a dash more milk if the dough feels dry. Carefully drop spoonfuls of the dough over the pork, cover again with foil and cook for a further 10 minutes. Remove the foil and cook for a further 5 minutes to brown the surface slightly.

For Cajun pork with cornmeal dumplings, make the dish as above, using 3 cored, deseeded and diced red peppers instead of the leeks and adding 4 teaspoons Cajun seasoning after the milk. For the dumplings, mix together 100 g (3½ oz) self-raising flour, 75 g (3 oz) cornmeal, 3 tablespoons chopped coriander and 50 g (2 oz) grated Cheddar cheese. Beat 1 egg with 75 ml (3 fl oz) milk and add to the bowl. Mix to a thick paste, adding a dash more milk if the mixture is dry. Use the dumpling mixture as above.

apple & cider pot-roasted pork

Serves **6**
Preparation time **25 minutes**
Cooking time **1¼ hours,**
  plus resting

1.5 kg (3 lb) **boned and rolled**
  leg of pork
4 tablespoons **vegetable oil**
several **rosemary sprigs**
1.25 kg (2½ lb) waxy
  potatoes, thickly sliced
2 large **dessert apples**
1 **onion,** sliced
175 ml (6 fl oz) **dry cider**
salt and **pepper**

Use a sharp knife or clean Stanley knife to score the skin of the pork at 1 cm (½ inch) intervals if it has not already been done. Sprinkle with salt and drizzle with 1 tablespoon of the oil then rub into the surface of the skin. Scatter the rosemary over the bottom of a roasting tin and sit the pork on top. Place on the lower rack of the halogen oven.

Set the temperature to 200°C (392°F) and cook for 45 minutes. While roasting, cook the potatoes in salted boiling water for 5 minutes until beginning to soften. Drain thoroughly and toss with the remaining oil.

Peel, core and thickly slice the apples. Scatter the apples and onion around the pork and pour over the cider. Arrange the potatoes on top and season to taste.

Return to the oven and cook for a further 30 minutes until the pork is cooked through and the potatoes are golden. Leave to rest for 20 minutes before serving with seasonal vegetables.

For maple-roasted pork with root vegetables, scatter a handful of sage leaves and parsley over the bottom of a roasting tin and place a 1.5 kg (3 lb) skinned, boned and rolled leg of pork on top. Drizzle with 2 tablespoons maple syrup and cook for 45 minutes. Cook 300 g (10 oz) baby carrots and 300 g (10 oz) small parsnips in boiling water for 3 minutes to soften. Scatter around the pork, along with 1 thinly sliced red onion. Drizzle the vegetables with 3 tablespoons maple syrup and 2 tablespoons vegetable oil and cook for a further 30 minutes until the vegetables are beginning to brown.

asian braised belly of pork

Serves **6**

Preparation time **20 minutes,**
   plus cooling
   and marinating

Cooking time about **2½ hours**
   10 minutes

1.25 kg (2½ lb) piece of
   boned pork belly, skin
   removed and trimmed of
   excess fat

2 **bay leaves**

100 ml (3½ fl oz) **rice vinegar**

100 g (3½ oz) **palm** or **light**
   muscovado sugar

2 tablespoons **salted black**
   beans

2 tablespoons **hoisin sauce**

4 tablespoons **dark soy sauce**

1 teaspoon freshly ground
   black pepper

2 **garlic cloves**, crushed

Put the piece of pork in a large saucepan and cover with water. Bring to the boil, reduce the heat and cook for 10 minutes. Leave to cool in the liquid, then drain, reserving the liquid. Score a crisscross pattern over the fatty side of the meat and cut into 6 portions. Place in a shallow glass or ceramic dish.

Mix together all the remaining ingredients and pour over the pork. Cover and leave to marinate in the refrigerator overnight.

Transfer the pork and its marinade to a casserole dish (or leave in the same dish if it is suitable) and place on the lower rack of the halogen oven. Lift the fat off the reserved broth and pour enough over the pork to just cover it.

Set the temperature to 250°C (482°F) and cook the pork for 10 minutes. Reduce the temperature to 150°C (302°F) and cook for about 2 hours until the pork is completely tender. Drain the pork and keep warm while finishing the sauce.

Pour the sauce into a saucepan and bring to the boil. Cook until reduced by about two-thirds. Serve with steamed rice and Asian greens.

For homemade hoisin sauce, in a bowl, mix together 5 tablespoons dark soy sauce, 3 tablespoons smooth peanut butter, 1½ tablespoons clear honey, 2 teaspoons rice vinegar, 2 teaspoons sesame oil and 2 teaspoons hot chilli sauce. Mix the ingredients thoroughly and store in a screw-top jar in the refrigerator for up to 3 weeks.

honey & mustard gammon

Serves **4**

Preparation time **5 minutes**

Cooking time **10 minutes**

4 **gammon steaks**,
   200–250 g (7–8 oz) each,
   trimmed of any excess fat

4 teaspoons **wholegrain
   mustard**

2 tablespoons **clear honey**

2 teaspoons **lemon juice**

1 tablespoon chopped
   tarragon

salt and **pepper**

Place the gammon steaks on the upper rack of the halogen oven.

Mix together the mustard, honey, lemon juice and tarragon in a bowl and season with a little salt and pepper. Brush a little of the mustard mixture over the steaks.

Set the temperature to 200°C (392°F) and cook the steaks for 5 minutes. Turn them over and brush with the remaining mustard mixture. Cook for a further 5 minutes or until the steaks are cooked through. Serve with chunky chips, a leafy salad and apple sauce.

For buttery homemade apple sauce to serve as an accompaniment, peel, core and chop 3 large cooking apples and put in a saucepan with 50 g (2 oz) butter, 40 g (1 ½ oz) caster sugar, 8 whole cloves, 1 tablespoon lemon juice and 2 tablespoons water. Cover and cook very gently for about 20 minutes until the apples are soft. Mash using a potato masher and turn into a serving dish. Serve warm or cold.

italian braised pork

Serves **4**
Preparation time **10 minutes**
Cooking time **1¾ hours,
    plus resting**

1 kg (2 lb) boned and rolled
    loin of pork
3 tablespoons **olive oil**
1 **fennel bulb**, thinly sliced
3 **garlic cloves**, crushed
1 teaspoon **fennel seeds**,
    lightly crushed
1 litre (1¾ pints) **milk**
salt and **pepper**

Season the pork with salt and pepper. Heat the oil in a frying pan on the hob and fry the pork on all sides to brown. Transfer the pork to a casserole dish in which it fits quite snugly.

Add the fennel to the pan and fry gently for 5 minutes to soften slightly. Add to the casserole along with the garlic, fennel seeds, milk and a little seasoning. Cover the dish with foil and place on the lower rack of the halogen oven.

Set the temperature to 150°C (302°F) and cook for 1½ hours or until the pork is tender. Drain the pork to a board or plate and leave to rest for 20 minutes. Pour the cooking juices into a saucepan and bring to the boil. Cook until the sauce has reduced to a creamy consistency. Serve with the pork.

For wilted spinach with pine nuts to serve as an accompaniment, heat 2 tablespoons olive oil in a wok or large frying pan and gently fry 40 g (1½ oz) pine nuts until beginning to colour. Drain with a slotted spoon and set aside. Scatter 3 tablespoons raisins into the pan with 2 finely chopped garlic cloves. Cook for 30 seconds, then add 400 g (13 oz) fresh spinach leaves and drizzle with 1 tablespoon water. Cook gently, turning the spinach with the garlic and raisins, until the spinach has just wilted. Lightly season with salt and pepper, and transfer to a serving dish. Serve sprinkled with the pine nuts.

pork kebabs in asian marinade

Serves **4**

Preparation time **15 minutes,**
   plus soaking and
   marinating

Cooking time **20 minutes**

3 tablespoons **medium sherry**
2 teaspoons **sesame oil**
2 teaspoons **five-spice**
   powder
1 teaspoon **ground ginger**
1 teaspoon **granulated sugar**
1 **garlic clove**, crushed
4 teaspoons **light soy sauce**
350 g (11½ oz) **pork fillet**, cut
   into 2.5 cm (1 inch) cubes
1 **red pepper**, cored,
   deseeded and cut into
   2.5 cm (1 inch) pieces
1 **red onion**, cut into
   2.5 cm (1 inch) pieces

Soak 8 bamboo skewers in cold water for several hours or overnight so that they do not burn during cooking.

Mix together the sherry, sesame oil, five-spice powder, ginger, sugar, garlic and soy sauce in a small lidded container or screw-top jar. Shake well to mix.

Put the pork in a polythene food bag and add the marinade. Turn to coat each piece, then transfer to the refrigerator to marinate for at least 2 hours or overnight.

Thread the pieces of pork, red pepper and onion alternately on to the skewers. Line the lower rack of the halogen oven with foil and arrange the skewers side by side on the foil.

Set the temperature to 200°C (392°F) and cook the kebabs for 18–20 minutes, turning once or twice, until the pork is cooked through. Serve the kebabs with steamed Thai fragrant rice, scattered with finely chopped spring onions.

For spice-rubbed pork skewers, crush together ½ teaspoon fennel seeds, ½ teaspoon cumin seeds, ½ teaspoon coriander seeds and ½ teaspoon black peppercorns, using either a mortar and pestle or a spice or coffee grinder. Mix in a bowl with 1 teaspoon finely chopped thyme and 1 tablespoon finely chopped coriander. Put 350 g (11½ oz) cubed pork fillet and the spice mixture in a polythene bag and turn to coat the pieces. Thread on to skewers as above, replacing the red pepper and red onion with white onion and lemon wedges and cook as above.

cranberry & juniper glazed pork

Serves **6**
Preparation time **10 minutes**
Cooking time **1 hour**
5 minutes, plus resting

1.5 kg (3 lb) skinned, boned
and rolled **leg of pork**
2 teaspoons **dried juniper
berries**
4 tablespoons **cranberry
sauce**
2 tablespoons **port**
150 ml (¼ pint) **chicken stock**
salt and **pepper**

Season the pork with salt and pepper, and place on the lower rack of the halogen oven.

Set the temperature to 200°C (392°F) and cook for 1 hour, turning the joint over after 20 minutes, then again after another 20 minutes.

Meanwhile, crush the juniper berries using a mortar and pestle, or use a small bowl and the end of a rolling pin. Tip into a bowl and stir in the cranberry sauce and port. Season with a little salt and pepper.

Brush half the glaze over the pork once you have turned the pork twice and there is 20 minutes' cooking time remaining. Finish cooking. Transfer the pork to a board or warm serving plate and leave to rest for 20 minutes.

Add the remaining glaze and the stock to the juices left in the base of the halogen oven and cook for 5 minutes or until heated through. Check the seasoning and pour into a small jug. Serve the pork cut into slices, with the sauce for pouring over and accompanied by roast potatoes and seasonal green vegetables.

For roast pork with orange & rosemary, blend the leaves from 3 rosemary sprigs in a spice or coffee grinder with 1 bay leaf, ½ teaspoon black peppercorns and ½ teaspoon celery salt. Rub over the surface of the pork joint and roast as above. After 40 minutes' cooking, brush the joint with 3 tablespoons orange marmalade; cook for the remaining time. Rest the meat as above while you make the gravy. Cook 150 ml (¼ pint) chicken stock and an additional 1 tablespoon orange marmalade with the juices in the base of the oven.

lamb

glazed rack of lamb

Serves **4**
Preparation time **10 minutes**
Cooking time **25 minutes,
    plus resting**

4 tablespoons **clear honey**
2 tablespoons **light soy sauce**
2 tablespoons **wholegrain
    mustard**
2 tablespoons chopped **mint**
2 **lean 6-bone racks of lamb**
salt and **pepper**

Mix together the honey, soy sauce, mustard and mint in a small bowl.

Season the lamb on both sides with salt and pepper. Brush all over with the honey mixture. Place the racks, fat-side uppermost, on a sheet of foil on the lower rack of the halogen oven.

Set the temperature to 200°C (392°F) and cook for 25 minutes, covering with foil if the lamb starts to brown too much. Leave to rest for 15 minutes before carving. Serve with roast potatoes and seasonal mixed vegetables, such as carrots and French beans.

For Parmesan & herb crusted lamb, season the lamb racks on both sides with salt and pepper as above and brush the fat sides with a little beaten egg. Mix together 40 g (1 ½ oz) dried breadcrumbs, 25 g (1 oz) grated Parmesan cheese, 1 chopped garlic clove, 2 tablespoons chopped parsley and 1 teaspoon chopped thyme. Season with salt and pepper. Spoon the breadcrumb mixture over the lamb and press down gently. Cook as above, covering with foil once the crust is golden.

lamb tikka kebabs

Serves **4**

Preparation time **20 minutes,
plus soaking and
marinating**

Cooking time **20 minutes**

150 ml (¼ pint) **natural yogurt**
juice of ½ **lemon**
1 **garlic clove**, crushed
1 tablespoon finely chopped
parsley
1 teaspoon **ground coriander**
½ teaspoon **ground turmeric**
1 teaspoon **chilli powder**
1 teaspoon **garam masala**
450 g (14½ oz) **lamb
tenderloin**, cut into 2.5cm
(1 inch) chunks
coriander sprigs, to garnish

Salad
1 **cucumber**, peeled, halved,
deseeded and diced
1 **garlic clove**, crushed
1 tablespoon chopped **mint**
1 teaspoon **caster sugar**
150 ml (¼ pint) **natural yogurt**

Soak 8 wooden skewers in cold water for several hours
or overnight so that they do not burn during cooking.

Mix together the yogurt, lemon juice, garlic, parsley,
coriander, turmeric, chilli powder and garam masala
in a large glass or ceramic bowl. Add the lamb and
stir to mix. Cover loosely and leave to marinate in the
refrigerator for at least 4 hours or overnight.

Thread the lamb on to the skewers and place on the
upper rack of the halogen oven.

Set the temperature to 225°C (437°F) and cook the
kebabs for about 20 minutes, turning them a couple
of times so that they cook evenly.

Meanwhile, in a bowl, mix together the salad
ingredients. Serve the salad with the kebabs and warm
naan or chapattis and lime wedges, garnished with
coriander sprigs.

For gingered lamb kebabs, grate 15 g (½ oz) fresh
root ginger into a large bowl and add 2 crushed garlic
cloves, 1 deseeded and finely chopped fresh red chilli,
1 tablespoon dark muscovado sugar and 2 tablespoons
dry sherry. Add the prepared lamb tenderloin as above
and leave to marinate in the refrigerator for at least
2 hours. Thread on to the soaked skewers and cook
as above.

lamb hot pot

Serves **2**
Preparation time **15 minutes**
Cooking time about **1 hour**

4 **lean lamb chops**, about
   100 g (3½ oz) each,
   trimmed of any excess fat
25 g (1 oz) **butter**
1 **onion**, thinly sliced
1 **garlic clove**, crushed
1 teaspoon chopped
   rosemary
2 **potatoes**, very thinly sliced
200 ml (7 fl oz) hot **lamb** or
   chicken stock
salt and **pepper**

Season the lamb chops lightly on both sides with salt and pepper.

Reserve a dot of the butter and melt the remainder in a frying pan on the hob. Fry the chops until lightly browned, then transfer to a shallow casserole dish. Add the onion, garlic and rosemary to the frying pan and fry gently for 3 minutes. Scatter over the lamb in the casserole.

Layer the potatoes on top and pour over the stock. Dot with the reserved butter, season lightly with salt and pepper and cover with foil. Place on the lower rack of the halogen oven.

Set the temperature to 200°C (392°F) and cook for 30–40 minutes until the potatoes are tender. Remove the foil and cook for a further 10 minutes until the surface is golden. Serve the hot pot with seasonal green vegetables.

For Mediterranean-style lamb hot pot, season and fry off the lamb as above, using 2 tablespoons olive oil instead of the butter, and transfer the lamb to the casserole dish. Add 2 thinly sliced courgettes and 1 sliced red onion to the frying pan and fry gently for 5 minutes, adding a dash more oil if needed. Add to the casserole. Omitting the potatoes, bring 200 ml (7 fl oz) lamb stock to the boil in the frying pan and stir in 2 tablespoons sun-dried tomato paste and 2 crushed garlic cloves. Add to the casserole and season lightly. Cover with foil and cook at the above temperature for 40–50 minutes.

summer roast lamb

Serves **6**

Preparation time **15 minutes,
plus marinating**

Cooking time **55 minutes,
plus resting**

2 tablespoons **olive oil**

3 tablespoons **red wine**

2 teaspoons **ground cumin**

2 teaspoons **hot paprika**

1 teaspoon coarsely ground
black pepper

1.5 kg (3 lb) **leg of lamb**

2 **garlic cloves**, thinly sliced

salt

Mix together the oil, wine, cumin, paprika and black pepper in a small bowl.

Place the lamb in a shallow dish and make small slits over the surface. Push a slice of garlic into each slit. Spoon over the spice mixture and spread it all over the lamb. Cover loosely with clingfilm and leave to marinate in the refrigerator for several hours, occasionally spooning the marinade over the meat. Place the lamb on the lower rack of the halogen oven.

Set the temperature to 250°C (482°F) and roast the lamb for 15 minutes. Reduce the temperature to 200°C (392°F) and roast for a further 40 minutes, spreading with the leftover marinade in the dish during cooking. (The lamb will be slightly pink in the centre; cook for a little longer if you prefer it well done.)

Transfer to a carving platter or board, and leave to rest for 20 minutes before carving. Serve with a Greek salad and warm pitta bread.

For a Greek salad to serve as an accompaniment, roughly chop 450 g (14½ oz) ripe tomatoes. Thinly slice 1 small red onion. Deseed and slice 1 cucumber. Put the ingredients in a salad bowl and scatter with 200 g (7 oz) roughly crumbled feta cheese and a handful of black olives. Mix 75 ml (3 fl oz) Greek olive oil with 1 tablespoon lemon juice and a little salt and pepper. Drizzle over the salad and sprinkle with 1 tablespoon finely chopped oregano.

slow-cooked aromatic lamb

Serves **6**

Preparation time **25 minutes, plus marinating**

Cooking time **1 hour**

750 g (1½ lb) **boned leg of lamb,** cut into 2 cm (¾ inch) cubes

3 **garlic cloves,** crushed

250 g (8 oz) **baby onions,** peeled and left whole

1 **red pepper,** cored, deseeded and cut into strips

2 tablespoons chopped **oregano**

1 teaspoon **dried basil**

2 **bay leaves**

300 ml (½ pint) **full-bodied red wine**

50 g (2 oz) **butter**

1 tablespoon **olive oil**

1 tablespoon **plain flour**

100 g (3½ oz) **button mushrooms**

salt and **pepper**

finely chopped **parsley,** to garnish

Put the lamb in a bowl and add the garlic, onions, red pepper, herbs and wine. Mix well. Cover loosely with clingfilm and marinate in the refrigerator overnight.

Drain off the liquid thoroughly from the lamb and vegetables; reserve the liquid. Pat the lamb and vegetables dry on kitchen paper. Melt 25 g (1 oz) of the butter with the oil in a large frying pan on the hob and fry the lamb, in batches, until browned. Transfer to a casserole dish. Gently fry the vegetables for 5 minutes and add to the casserole.

Melt the remaining butter in the frying pan and add the flour, stirring to make a paste. Gradually whisk in the reserved liquid and bring to the boil. Pour into the casserole dish and cover with foil. Place on the lower rack of the halogen oven.

Set the temperature to 200°C (392°F) and cook for 30 minutes. Stir in the mushrooms and cook for a further 20 minutes or until the lamb is tender. Check the seasoning, adding salt and pepper if needed, and sprinkle with finely chopped parsley. Serve with mashed potato, saffron risotto or polenta.

For creamy polenta to serve as an accompaniment, bring 1 litre (1¾ pints) water to the boil in a large saucepan. Gradually tip in 225 g (7½ oz) quick-cook polenta, whisking continuously to eliminate any lumps. Continue to cook the polenta over a gentle heat for about 5–10 minutes, stirring with a wooden spoon, until the mixture is smooth and thickened. Stir in 50 g (2 oz) butter, 25 g (1 oz) grated Parmesan cheese and plenty of salt and pepper. Serve with the lamb.

easy lamb curry

Serves **2**

Preparation time **10 minutes**

Cooking time **35 minutes**

25 g (1 oz) **butter**

2 tablespoons **vegetable oil**

350 g (11½ oz) **lean boneless lamb**, diced

1 **onion**, sliced

2 **garlic cloves**, chopped

1 **cinnamon stick**, halved

6 **cardamom pods**, crushed to open

1 teaspoon **ground cumin**

1 teaspoon **ground ginger**

1 teaspoon **chilli powder**

2 teaspoons **garam masala**

250 ml (8 fl oz) **water**

salt

finely chopped coriander to garnish

Melt the butter with the oil in a frying pan on the hob and fry the diced lamb until browned. Transfer to a casserole dish.

Add the onion to the pan and fry gently for 5 minutes. Stir in the garlic and spices. Season with salt and fry for a further 2 minutes. Stir in the measurement water and bring just to the boil. Pour over the lamb. Place on the lower rack of the halogen oven.

Set the temperature to 200°C (392°F) and cook for 20 minutes until the lamb is tender, stirring twice. Serve with basmati rice, garnished with finely chopped coriander.

For speedy lamb with peppers, heat 2 tablespoons olive oil in a frying pan on the hob and fry 350 g (11½ oz) lean diced boneless lamb, 1 small sliced red onion and 2 cored, deseeded and sliced red peppers for 5 minutes. Tip into a shallow ovenproof dish and place on the upper rack of the halogen oven. Set the temperature to 200°C (392°F) and cook for 15 minutes, stirring twice. Meanwhile, mix together 1 tablespoon clear honey, 1 tablespoon tomato purée, 1 tablespoon Worcestershire sauce, 1 tablespoon orange juice, 1 teaspoon sweet chilli sauce and ½ teaspoon cornflour. Add to the meat, stirring to mix. Cook for a further 5 minutes.

navarin of lamb

Serves **6**
Preparation time **25 minutes**
Cooking time **1 hour
40 minutes**

2 tablespoons **plain flour**
1.5 kg (3 lb) **boned shoulder
of lamb**, trimmed of any
excess fat and cut into
small chunks
50 g (2 oz) **butter**
1 tablespoon **olive oil**
2 **onions**, sliced
900 ml (1 ½ pints) **lamb** or
chicken stock
4 **garlic cloves**, crushed
3 **bay leaves**
several **thyme sprigs**
2 tablespoons **tomato purée**
250 g (8 oz) **baby carrots**
250 g (8 oz) **baby turnips**
250 g (8 oz) **French beans**
200 g (7 oz) **fresh peas**
salt and **pepper**

Season the flour with salt and pepper, and use to coat the lamb.

Melt half the butter with the oil in a large frying pan on the hob and fry the lamb, in batches, until browned. Transfer the browned meat to the bowl of the halogen oven. Add the onions to the frying pan and fry gently for a few minutes to soften. Pour in the stock and add the garlic, herbs and tomato purée. Season with a little salt and pepper. Bring just to the boil, then tip the contents of the pan over the meat in the bowl of the oven. Stir the ingredients together.

Set the temperature to 200°C (392°F) and cook for 1 hour until the lamb is tender.

Meanwhile, towards the end of the cooking time, melt the remaining butter in a frying pan and gently fry the carrots and turnips for 5 minutes to soften. Cook the beans in boiling water for 3 minutes.

Add all the vegetables to the bowl and cook for a further 20 minutes or until tender. Check the seasoning and serve in bowls with grainy bread or new potatoes.

For saffron-spiced lamb, prepare the casserole as above, replacing the thyme with 1 halved cinnamon stick and sprinkling in 1 teaspoon crumbled saffron threads. Cook as above for one hour. Chop 75 g (3 oz) ready-to-eat dried apricots into pieces. Add to the casserole along with a drained 400 g (13 oz) can chickpeas and a handful of chopped coriander, instead of the spring vegetables and cook for a further 20 minutes.

lamb & tomato couscous

Serves **6**
Preparation time **20 minutes**
Cooking time **1 hour**

450 g (14½ oz) **lamb
tenderloin**, cut into
small chunks
3 tablespoons **olive oil**
2 **onions**, sliced
4 small **carrots**, sliced
1 **green pepper**, cored,
deseeded and cut into
small chunks
2 **garlic cloves**, crushed
400 g (13 oz) **can chopped
tomatoes**
2 teaspoons **light muscovado
sugar**
1 teaspoon **ground turmeric**
1 teaspoon **ground coriander**
1 teaspoon **ground cumin**
1 teaspoon **chilli powder**
100 g (3½ oz) **pitted dates**,
chopped
300 g (10 oz) **instant
couscous**
2 teaspoons **vegetable
bouillon powder**
425 ml (15 fl oz) **boiling water**
salt and **pepper**

Season the lamb with salt and pepper. Heat the oil in a frying pan on the hob and fry the lamb until browned. Transfer to a casserole dish.

Add the onions, carrots and green pepper to the pan and fry for 5 minutes to soften. Stir in the garlic, tomatoes, sugar and spices. Season with a little salt and pepper. Bring to the boil, then tip the contents of the pan into the casserole dish. Stir in the dates. Cover the casserole dish with foil and place on the lower rack of the halogen oven.

Set the temperature to 200°C (392°F) and cook for 45 minutes or until the lamb is tender.

Meanwhile, towards the end of the cooking time, put the couscous and bouillon powder in a heatproof bowl, stir to mix and pour over the measurement boiling water. Cover and leave to stand for 10 minutes until the water has been absorbed. Fluff up the couscous with a fork and serve with the lamb.

For Greek lamb casserole, prepare and fry off the lamb and vegetables as above, using 1 diced aubergine instead of the carrots. Replace the spices with 3 bay leaves, several thyme sprigs and 1 teaspoon crumbled dried oregano, and the dates with a handful of roughly chopped pitted black olives. While cooking, stir 1 tablespoon finely chopped mint and a crushed garlic clove into 200 g (7 oz) Greek yogurt. Serve the casserole in bowls, topped with spoonfuls of the yogurt and accompanied by warm pitta bread.

roast stuffed shoulder of lamb

Serves **6**
Preparation time **20 minutes**
Cooking time **1¾ hours,
    plus resting**

2 **garlic cloves**, crushed
2 tablespoons **olive oil**
1.5 kg (3 lb) **boned shoulder
    of lamb**
100 g (3½ oz) **bread**, cut into
    small dice
50 g (2 oz) **butter**
1 **onion**, chopped
4 **celery sticks**, chopped
4 tablespoons chopped
    parsley
½ teaspoon **cayenne pepper**
200 ml (7 fl oz) **red wine**
2 tablespoons **clear honey**
salt and **pepper**

Mix together the garlic and oil with a little salt and pepper. Brush over the lamb. Cover and chill.

Spread the bread out on a baking sheet and place on the upper rack of the halogen oven. Set the temperature to 250°C (482°F) and cook for about 5 minutes until toasted, watching closely so that the bread does not brown too much.

Melt the butter in a frying pan on the hob and fry the onion and celery for 5 minutes to soften. Tip into a bowl and stir in the toasted bread, parsley, cayenne and a little salt. Lay the lamb on a board, skin-side down, and pack the stuffing into the cavity. Secure the ends with skewers to hold the stuffing in place. Place the lamb on the lower rack of the halogen oven and cover with foil.

Set the temperature to 250°C (482°F) and cook for 15 minutes. Reduce the temperature to 200°C (392°F) and cook for a further 1 hour until tender. Remove the foil and cook for 15 minutes to colour the surface. Transfer to a board and leave to rest for 20 minutes before carving.

Meanwhile, skim off the fat from the bowl of the oven and add the red wine and honey. Season with salt and pepper. Cook for 5 minutes until the gravy is hot. Transfer to a jug and serve with the lamb.

For tapenade-stuffed lamb, brush the lamb with the garlic-flavoured oil. Fry 1 chopped onion and 1 cored, deseeded and chopped green pepper in 3 tablespoons olive oil until soft. Add 50 g (2 oz) fresh white bread-crumbs and 75 ml (3 fl oz) black olive tapenade. Stir to combine. Use to stuff the lamb. Continue as above.

spring lamb casserole

Serves **4**
Preparation time **20 minutes**
Cooking time **55 minutes**

1 tablespoon **plain flour**
675 g (1 lb 6 oz) **lean boned
leg of lamb**, cut into
small pieces
50 g (2 oz) **butter**
finely grated rind of 1 **lemon**
2 **garlic cloves**, crushed
1 bunch of **spring onions**,
sliced
150 ml (¼ pint) **white wine**
or **cider**
450 ml (¾ pint) **lamb** or
chicken stock
2 **bay leaves**
2 **courgettes**, sliced
75 g (3 oz) **cauliflower florets**
75 g (3 oz) **sugarsnap peas**
2 tablespoons chopped **mint**
salt and **pepper**

Season the flour with salt and pepper, and use to coat
the lamb.

Melt half the butter in a large frying pan on the hob and
fry the lamb, in batches, until browned, transferring the
browned pieces to a casserole dish. Add the lemon rind,
garlic and spring onions to the casserole.

Pour the wine or cider and the stock into the frying
pan and add the bay leaves and a little salt and pepper.
Bring to the boil, then tip the contents of the pan into
the casserole. Cover with foil and place on the lower
rack of the halogen oven.

Set the temperature to 200°C (392°F) and cook for
30 minutes.

Meanwhile, melt the remaining butter in the frying pan
and gently fry the courgettes and cauliflower for
5 minutes. Add to the casserole with the sugarsnap
peas and mint. Cook for a further 15 minutes or until
both meat and vegetables are tender. Serve with
buttered new potatoes.

For lamb casserole with rosemary dumplings,

mix together 150 g (5 oz) self-raising flour, 75 g
(3 oz) shredded beef or vegetable suet and 2 teaspoons
chopped rosemary. Season with salt and pepper. Add
125 ml (4 fl oz) water and bring together into a dough.
Prepare the casserole as above and cook for 30
minutes. Stir in 100 ml (3½ fl oz) double cream and
150 g (5 oz) broad beans instead of the cauliflower and
sugarsnap peas, then add the mint and place spoonfuls
of the dumpling mixture on top. Cover with foil and cook
for 15 minutes, until the dumplings are risen and fluffy.

honeyed lamb shanks

Serves **4**
Preparation time **15 minutes**
Cooking time **1½ hours**

1 tablespoon **plain flour**
4 **lamb shanks**, about 400 g
   (13 oz) each
25 g (1 oz) **butter**
1 tablespoon **olive oil**
6 **shallots**, thinly sliced
5 **garlic cloves**, thinly sliced
finely grated rind of **1 orange**
200 ml (7 fl oz) **red wine**
400 ml (14 fl oz) **lamb** or
   chicken stock
2 tablespoons **Worcestershire
   sauce**
3 tablespoons **clear honey**
1 teaspoon **cayenne pepper**
several **rosemary sprigs**
500 g (1 lb) **new potatoes**
400 g (14 oz) **can flageolet
   beans**, rinsed and drained
salt and **pepper**

Season the flour with salt and pepper, and use to
coat the lamb shanks. Melt the butter with the oil in
a frying pan on the hob and fry the lamb on all sides
for about 10 minutes until browned. Transfer to the
bowl of the halogen oven.

Add the shallots to the frying pan and fry for
3 minutes. Stir in the garlic, orange rind, wine, stock,
Worcestershire sauce, honey, cayenne and rosemary.
Bring to the boil and pour over the lamb.

Set the temperature to 200°C (392°F) and cook
for 1 hour, turning the shanks several times during
cooking. Meanwhile, cook the potatoes in salted
boiling water for 5 minutes. Drain and add to the oven
with the beans. Cook for a further 15 minutes until
both lamb and potatoes are tender. Check the
seasoning before serving.

For lamb shanks with lemon & capers, fry off the
lamb shanks and other ingredients as above, replacing
the red wine with 200 ml (7 fl oz) white wine, the
orange rind with the finely grated rind of 1 lemon
and the Worcestershire sauce and cayenne with
2 tablespoons rinsed and drained capers. Cook as
above for 1¼. Finely chop 1 large garlic clove and mix
with the grated rind of 1 lemon and 2 tablespoons
chopped parsley to make gremolata. Check the
casserole for seasoning and serve scattered with
the gremolata.

seafood

honey & sesame salmon

Serves **2**
Preparation time **10 minutes**
Cooking time **12 minutes**

1 tablespoon **clear honey**
1 tablespoon **light soy sauce**
sunflower oil, for oiling
2 plump **salmon fillets**, about
150 g (5 oz) each
2 **spring onions**, finely
chopped
2 tablespoons **sesame seeds**

Mix together the honey and soy sauce in a small bowl.

Oil a sheet of foil lightly and arrange the salmon fillets, side by side, on the foil. Brush with the honey mixture and sprinkle first with the spring onions, then the sesame seeds. Place the foil on the upper rack of the halogen oven.

Set the temperature to 225°C (437°F) and cook for 10–12 minutes until the salmon is cooked through. (Test by piercing the plumpest area of the flesh with a knife – the flesh should flake easily.) Serve with buttered new potatoes and a rocket salad.

For salmon with tarragon cream sauce, arrange the salmon fillets on the oiled sheet of foil as above. Place a knob of butter on top of each fillet, season lightly with salt and pepper and cook as above. While cooking, melt 15 g (½ oz) butter in a small saucepan and stir in 15 g (½ oz) plain flour until mixed. Gradually blend in 300 ml (½ pint) fish stock, ¼ teaspoon curry paste and the leaves from several sprigs of tarragon. Bring to the boil and cook until slightly thickened. Stir in 2 tablespoons crème fraîche and season to taste before serving with the salmon.

malaysian prawn curry

Serves **4**
Preparation time **25 minutes**
Cooking time **35 minutes**

2 tablespoons **vegetable oil**
2 **onions**, sliced
3 cm (1¼ inch) piece of **fresh
  root ginger**, finely chopped
2 **garlic cloves**, crushed
2 teaspoons **cumin seeds**,
  crushed
2 teaspoons **coriander seeds**,
  crushed
1 teaspoon **dried chilli flakes**
good pinch of **ground cloves**
1 **cinnamon stick**
500 ml (17 fl oz) **fish** or
  vegetable stock
2 tablespoons **lime juice**
1 tablespoon **light
  muscovado sugar**
2 tablespoons **light soy sauce**
1 **green pepper**, cored,
  deseeded and diced
4 teaspoons **cornflour**
225 g (7½ oz) can **pineapple
  slices** in natural juice,
  drained (reserve the juice)
400 g (13 oz) peeled and
  deveined raw **prawns**
salt

Heat the oil in a large frying pan or wok on the hob and fry the onions for about 8 minutes until beginning to brown. Stir in the ginger, garlic, cumin and coriander seeds, chilli flakes, cloves and cinnamon, and cook for a further 2 minutes.

Pour in the stock and add the lime juice, sugar, soy sauce and green pepper. Bring almost to the boil. Pour the contents of the pan into a casserole dish and cover with foil. Place on the lower rack of the halogen oven. Set the temperature to 225°C (437°F) and cook for 15 minutes.

Meanwhile, blend the cornflour with 4 tablespoons of the reserved pineapple juice in a small bowl. Chop the pineapple slices and add to the casserole along with the cornflour mixture and the prawns. Cook, uncovered, for a further 10 minutes or until the sauce has thickened and the prawns are pink and cooked through. Serve with steamed rice or sesame noodles.

For sesame noodles to serve as an accompaniment, fry 2 finely chopped shallots in 1 tablespoon vegetable oil until softened. Add 300 g (10 oz) straight-to-wok medium or thread noodles, 2 tablespoons sesame oil and 2 tablespoons rice vinegar. Cook, stirring, until heated through. Transfer to a serving dish and scatter with chopped coriander and toasted sesame seeds.

red mullet with pomegranate

Serves **4**
Preparation time **15 minutes**
Cooking time **8 minutes**

8 large **red mullet fillets**,
  about
  75 g (3 oz) each
8 **rosemary sprigs**
finely grated rind and juice of
  1 **lime**
2 teaspoons **clear honey**
2 tablespoons **olive oil**
seeds of 1 **pomegranate**
salt and **pepper**

Use a sharp knife to make several shallow diagonal cuts through the fish fillets.

Arrange the rosemary sprigs in a layer across the bottom of a shallow ovenproof dish and place the fillets, skin-side up, on top.

Mix together the lime rind and juice, honey, olive oil and a little salt and pepper in a small bowl, and brush over the fish. Place the ovenproof dish on the upper rack of the halogen oven.

Set the temperature to 250°C (482°F) and cook the fillets for about 8 minutes until cooked through. (Test by piercing the thickest area of the flesh with the tip of a knife – the flesh should flake easily.) Scatter the pomegranate seeds into the dish to serve.

For a couscous salad to serve as an accompaniment, put 250 g (8 oz) instant couscous in a heatproof bowl and add 300 ml (½ pint) hot chicken or vegetable stock. Cover and leave to stand for about 10 minutes until the couscous has plumped up and absorbed the stock. Leave to cool, then fluff up the grains with a fork and stir in 2 tablespoons chopped mint, 2 tablespoons chopped parsley, 50 g (2 oz) chopped shelled pistachio nuts, 50 g (2 oz) raisins, 2 tablespoons olive oil and 1 tablespoon white wine vinegar. Season to taste with salt and pepper.

fish kebabs with garlic butter

Serves **4**
Preparation time **25 minutes,
  plus marinating**
Cooking time **15 minutes**

450 g (14½ oz) **cod fillet,**
  skinned and cut into
  bite-sized chunks
75 g (3 oz) **thinly sliced
  pancetta,** halved
8 small **tomatoes**
200 g (7 oz) **chestnut
  mushrooms**
1 **red pepper,** cored,
  deseeded and cut
  into chunks
100 g (3½ oz) **butter**
1 tablespoon **olive oil**
finely grated rind of 1 **lemon**
2 **garlic cloves,** crushed
1 tablespoon chopped **parsley**
1 tablespoon chopped **thyme**
salt and **pepper**

Wrap the fish chunks in the pieces of pancetta. Using a sharp knife, cut a small cross in the base of each tomato. Thread the pancetta-wrapped cod, tomatoes, mushrooms and red pepper chunks alternately on to the soaked wooden skewers. Place in a shallow ovenproof dish.

Melt 25 g (1 oz) of the butter with the oil in a saucepan, stir in the lemon rind and season with a little salt and pepper. Brush over the kebabs and leave to marinate in the refrigerator for about 1 hour. Place the kebab dish on the upper rack of the halogen oven.

Set the temperature to 250°C (482°F) and cook the kebabs for 10–15 minutes, turning them once or twice, until cooked through.

Meanwhile, melt the remaining butter in the pan and stir in the garlic, parsley and thyme. Season lightly and serve spooned over the kebabs, accompanied by rustic bread for mopping up the juices.

For sauce vierge to serve instead of the garlic butter, skin 4 tomatoes and scoop out the seeds. Chop the flesh into small dice. Put 100 ml (3½ fl oz) olive oil in a small saucepan and stir in ½ teaspoon crushed coriander seeds, ½ teaspoon crushed cumin seeds, a small handful of chopped herbs such as parsley, chervil, tarragon and chives, 1 crushed garlic clove, a little seasoning and the chopped tomatoes. Warm through gently before serving with the kebabs.

apricot & honey stuffed mackerel

Serves **4**
Preparation time **15 minutes**
Cooking time **25 minutes**

50 g (2 oz) plump **ready-to-eat dried apricots**, chopped
50 g (2 oz) **cooked bulgar wheat**
2 tablespoons **clear honey**
1 **garlic clove**, crushed
2 tablespoons chopped **tarragon**
2 teaspoons chopped **mint**
50 g (2 oz) butter, plus extra for greasing
4 small whole **mackerel**, gutted and cleaned
150 ml (¼ pint) **dry white wine**
2 tablespoons **double cream**
salt and **pepper**
chopped **parsley**, to garnish

Mix the apricots in a bowl with the bulgar wheat, honey, garlic, tarragon and mint, and season with salt and pepper. Fill the fish cavities with the stuffing and tie 2 lengths of kitchen string around each fish to hold the stuffing in place.

Place the fish, side by side, in a buttered shallow ovenproof dish. Pour over the wine and dot with the butter. Cover with foil and place on the lower rack of the halogen oven.

Set the temperature to 200°C (392°F) and cook for 20–25 minutes until cooked through, removing the foil for the last few minutes of the cooking time. Swirl the cream into the juices and serve sprinkled with parsley, accompanied by lemon wedges.

For baked mackerel with citrus butter, melt
15 g (½ oz) butter in a frying pan on the hob and add ½ teaspoon crushed fennel seeds. Cook for 30 seconds, then remove from the heat and turn into a bowl. Add a further 75 g (3 oz) softened butter to the bowl, plus the finely grated rind of ½ orange and 1 lemon, 2 tablespoons snipped chives and plenty of pepper. Beat well to mix. Turn into a small dish and chill. Score each of the four mackerel in about 3 places on both sides to allow the flavours to soak in. Season with salt and pepper. Put the fish in a shallow ovenproof dish, dot with 50 g (2 oz) butter and cook as above. Serve with the flavoured butter spooned over.

family fish pie

Serves **4**

Preparation time **30 minutes**

Cooking time **55 minutes**

1 kg (2 lb) **floury potatoes**

625 g (1 ¼ lb) **cod**, **pollack** or
haddock fillet, skinned

600 ml (1 pint) **milk**

100 g (3½ oz) **butter**

1 **onion**, finely chopped

2 **celery sticks**, thinly sliced

2 tablespoons chopped
parsley

40 g (1½ oz) **plain flour**

100 g (3½ oz) **mature**
Cheddar cheese, grated

100 ml (3½ fl oz) **single**
cream or **milk**

salt and **pepper**

Cook the potatoes in salted boiling water for
20 minutes or until tender. Drain and set aside.

Meanwhile, put the fish in a shallow ovenproof dish
with half the milk. Place on the lower rack of the
halogen oven. Set the temperature to 250°C (482°F)
and cook for 20 minutes until the fish is cooked
through. Drain off the milk, reserving it for the sauce,
and flake the fish evenly over the bottom of the dish.

Melt 25 g (1 oz) of the butter in a saucepan and gently
fry the onion and celery for about 5 minutes until
softened. Spoon the onion and celery mixture over
the flaked fish and scatter with the parsley.

Melt a further 50 g (2 oz) of the butter in a clean
saucepan and stir in the flour to make a smooth paste.
Remove from the heat and gradually blend in all the
reserved milk. Return to the heat and bring to the boil,
stirring constantly, until thickened. Stir in half the cheese
and season to taste with salt and pepper.

Spoon half the sauce over the fish. Mash the potatoes
with the cream, remaining butter and seasoning, and
add to the dish, spreading evenly. Scatter with the
remaining cheese and place on the lower rack of the
halogen oven. Set the temperature to 200°C (392°F)
and cook for 20–25 minutes until the surface is golden.

For spiced smoked haddock pie, replace the white
fish fillets with 625 g (1 ¼ lb) skinned smoked haddock
fillets and add 4 halved hard-boiled eggs to the fish.
Replace the parsley with 2 tablespoons chopped
coriander and add 1 tablespoon medium curry paste
to the thickened sauce. Finish as above.

spicy crab cakes

Serves **6**
Preparation time **30 minutes plus cooling**
Cooking time **12 minutes**

1 tablespoon **vegetable oil**, plus a little extra for drizzling
½ bunch of **spring onions**, thinly sliced, plus extra, cut into strips and dropped into cold water to make curls, to garnish
2 **garlic cloves**, crushed
1 fresh **red chilli**, deseeded and finely chopped
350 g (11½ oz) **crabmeat**
2 teaspoons **tomato ketchup**
4 tablespoons **mayonnaise**
2 teaspoons **Worcestershire sauce**
175 g (6 oz) **dried breadcrumbs**
50 g (2 oz) **plain flour**
1 **egg**
salt and **pepper**

Heat the oil in a frying pan on the hob and gently fry the sliced spring onions for 2 minutes. Stir in the garlic and chilli, then tip the contents of the pan into a bowl. Leave to cool.

Add the crabmeat, ketchup, mayonnaise, Worcestershire sauce and 50 g (2 oz) of the breadcrumbs to the bowl, season with a little salt and pepper and stir well to mix. Shape the mixture into 12 cakes.

Season the flour with salt and pepper on a plate. Beat the egg on a second plate and scatter the remaining breadcrumbs on a third. Dust the fishcakes with the flour, then coat in the egg and breadcrumbs.

Drizzle a little extra oil into a shallow roasting tin and space the fishcakes slightly apart in the tin. (You may need to cook them in 2 batches.) Drizzle with more oil and place on the upper rack of the halogen oven.

Set the temperature to 200°C (392°F) and cook the fishcakes for 8–10 minutes, turning over halfway through cooking. Serve with extra mayonnaise or sweet chilli sauce, scattered with spring onion curls.

For homemade mayonnaise, put 2 egg yolks, 2 teaspoons Dijon mustard, 1 tablespoon white wine vinegar and a little salt and pepper in a food processor and process lightly to mix. Pour 250 ml (8 fl oz) sunflower or light olive oil (or a mixture) into a jug. With the machine running, trickle in the oil in a steady stream until the mayonnaise is thick and glossy. Don't add the oil too quickly or it may separate. Turn into a jar and refrigerate for up to 3 days.

mediterranean roast monkfish

Serves **4**

Preparation time **10 minutes**

Cooking time **25 minutes**

2 small **fennel bulbs**,
   thinly sliced

1 **red onion**, thinly sliced

1 large **courgette**, thinly sliced

4 tablespoons **olive oil**

2 tablespoons chopped
   oregano

1 tablespoon chopped **thyme**

12 **black olives**

4 pieces of **monkfish fillet**,
   about 175 g (6 oz) each

4 **canned anchovy**
   fillets, drained (reserve
   2 tablespoons of their
   preserving oil)

2 **garlic cloves**, crushed

salt and **pepper**

basil leaves, to garnish
   (**optional**)

Put the fennel, onion, courgette and olive oil in a shallow roasting tin and mix together, seasoning with salt and pepper. Place on the upper rack of the halogen oven.

Set the temperature to 200°C (392°F) and cook for 10 minutes, stirring a couple of times, until the vegetables have softened. Stir in the herbs and olives.

Season the monkfish fillets with salt and pepper, and nestle them down into the vegetables. Mash the drained anchovy fillets in a bowl, then add their oil, the garlic and a little seasoning. Spoon the dressing over the fish. Cook for about 15 minutes until the monkfish is cooked through. Serve scattered with basil leaves.

For sardines with chilli tomatoes, slice 6 tomatoes and scatter in a shallow roasting tin. Mix 2 tablespoons chilli oil with 2 tablespoons sun-dried tomato paste and drizzle over the top. Remove the heads from 8 gutted and cleaned fresh sardines and arrange over the tomatoes. Scatter with 1 tablespoon rinsed and drained capers and a little salt. Place on the lower rack of the halogen oven and roast at 200°C (392°F) for about 25 minutes until the sardines are cooked through. Serve scattered with coriander leaves.

salmon & watercress sauce

Serves **2**

Preparation time **10 minutes**

Cooking time **10 minutes**

2 **thick salmon fillets**, about
175 g (6 oz) each

2 tablespoons **olive oil**, plus
extra for oiling

25 g (1 oz) **butter**

2 **shallots**, chopped

1 teaspoon **plain flour**

75 ml (3 fl oz) **vegetable
stock**

40 g (1½ oz) **watercress**,
tough stalks removed, plus
extra sprigs for garnishing

3 tablespoons **double cream**

freshly grated **nutmeg**

salt and **pepper**

Put the salmon fillets in a lightly oiled shallow ovenproof dish and drizzle with the olive oil. Season lightly with salt and pepper, and place the dish on the upper rack of the halogen oven.

Set the temperature to 225°C (437°F) and bake for 10 minutes or until just cooked through. (Test by piercing the thickest area with the tip of a knife – the flesh should flake easily.)

Meanwhile, melt the butter in a saucepan until bubbling. Add the shallots and fry gently for 3 minutes. Sprinkle in the flour and cook, stirring, for 1 minute. Remove from the heat and gradually blend in the stock, then the watercress. Return to the heat and cook gently for 2 minutes, stirring, until thickened.

Pour the sauce into a food processor and process until smooth, or push through a sieve. Return to the rinsed-out pan and stir in the cream, nutmeg and salt and pepper to taste. Serve with the salmon, garnished with watercress sprigs, and accompany with buttered new potatoes.

For dill & mustard sauce to serve instead of watercress sauce, pull the thick stalks from 5 g (¼ oz) dill and chop the dill finely. Put 1 tablespoon wholegrain mustard in a small bowl with a dash of Tabasco sauce, 1 tablespoon caster sugar and a pinch of salt. Whisking constantly, gradually add 75 ml (3 fl oz) light olive oil in a thin, steady stream until the sauce is thickened and smooth. Beat in the dill and turn into a small serving jug.

trout with almonds

Serves **2**
Preparation time **5 minutes**
Cooking time **15 minutes**

2 small **whole trout,** gutted
  and cleaned
plain flour, for dusting
65 g (2½ oz) **butter**
3 tablespoons **flaked
  almonds**
salt and **pepper**

Score the trout several times down each side. Season the flour with salt and pepper, and use to lightly dust the trout. Place in a shallow ovenproof dish.

Melt the butter and drizzle over the trout so that they are completely coated. Scatter with the almonds and place on the lower rack of the halogen oven.

Set the temperature to 225°C (437°F) and bake the trout for about 15 minutes until cooked through. (Test by piercing a thick area of the fish with the tip of a knife – the flesh should flake easily.) Serve with lemon or lime wedges and seasonal vegetables.

For bacon-wrapped trout with tarragon, score the trout several times down each side and pack plenty of tarragon and chives into the cavities. Wrap 2 thinly sliced streaky bacon rashers around each fish and place in a shallow ovenproof dish. Drizzle with 25 g (1 oz) melted butter and season with plenty of pepper. Cook as above.

vegetarian

cauliflower cheese

Serves **2**
Preparation time **10 minutes**
Cooking time **15 minutes**

½ **cauliflower**, about 500 g
  (1 lb), cut into large florets
300 ml (½ pint) **ready-made**
  béchamel sauce
1 teaspoon **Dijon mustard**
1 tablespoon chopped **dill** or
  tarragon
50 g (2 oz) **mature Cheddar**
  cheese, grated
salt and **pepper**

Put the cauliflower in a saucepan of salted boiling water on the hob. Cook for 4–5 minutes until tender. Drain and scatter in a shallow ovenproof dish.

Heat the béchamel sauce in a small saucepan and stir in the mustard, dill or tarragon and half the Cheddar. Season to taste with salt and pepper. Spoon over the cauliflower and sprinkle with the remaining cheese. Place on the upper rack of the halogen oven.

Set the temperature to 225°C (437°F) and cook for about 10 minutes until the cheese is melting and pale golden. Serve hot.

For homemade sauce with cheese, put 150 ml (¼ pint) milk in a saucepan with 1 small chopped onion, 1 bay leaf and several peppercorns. Bring to the boil, remove from the heat and leave to stand for 15 minutes. Strain through a sieve. Melt 15 g (½ oz) butter in a small saucepan and stir in 1 tablespoon plain flour. Cook gently, stirring, for 1 minute. Remove from the heat and gradually blend in the milk. Return to the heat and cook gently, stirring, until the sauce is thickened. Stir in 40 g (1½ oz) finely grated mature Cheddar cheese until the cheese has melted and the sauce is smooth and glossy.

pumpkin & green chilli curry

Serves **4**
Preparation time **20 minutes plus standing**
Cooking time **35 minutes**

flesh of ½ **coconut**, chopped into small pieces
275 ml (9 fl oz) **very hot water**
2.5 cm (1 inch) piece of **fresh root ginger**, chopped
3 **garlic cloves**, chopped
½ teaspoon **ground turmeric**
1 tablespoon **caster sugar**
1 tablespoon **lime juice**
750 g (1 ½ lb) **pumpkin**, peeled, deseeded and cut into small chunks
2 **fresh green chillies**, deseeded and thinly sliced
25 g (1 oz) **butter**
1 large **onion**, thinly sliced
2 tablespoons **toasted pumpkin seeds**
salt (optional)

Tip the coconut into a food processor with the measurement of hot water. Process until the coconut is finely grated. Transfer to a bowl and leave to stand for 10 minutes.

Put the ginger, garlic, turmeric, sugar and lime juice in the food processor. Strain the coconut-infused water through a sieve and add the liquid to the processor, discarding the pulp. Process until smooth.

Scatter the pumpkin in a casserole dish. Add the chillies and pour in the coconut mixture from the processor. Cover with foil and place on the lower rack of the halogen oven.

Set the temperature to 200°C (392°F) and cook for about 30 minutes until the pumpkin is tender. While cooking, melt the butter in a frying pan on the hob and gently fry the onion for 8–10 minutes until very soft. Stir into the curry and cook for a further 5 minutes. Check the seasoning, adding salt if needed, and scatter with the pumpkin seeds. Serve with plain or flavoured warm naan bread and mango chutney.

For mango & coriander chutney to serve as an accompaniment, dice the flesh of 2 small ripe mangoes and place in a bowl. Crush 12 cardamom pods using a mortar and pestle, and remove the husks. Crush the seeds a little more and tip into a frying pan. Add 2 finely chopped shallots, a good pinch of cayenne pepper and 1 teaspoon vegetable or wok oil. Cook very gently until the shallots have softened. Add to the mango with a handful of chopped coriander and 150 ml (¼ pint) natural yogurt. Stir, refrigerate and eat the same day.

chickpea & pepper chilli

Serves **4**
Preparation time **20 minutes**
Cooking time **1 hour**

3 tablespoons **olive oil**
1 large **onion**, chopped
2 **celery sticks**, chopped
2 **courgettes**, chopped
2 **red peppers**, cored,
   deseeded and chopped
3 **garlic cloves**, crushed
2 teaspoons **dried oregano**
2 teaspoons **cumin seeds**,
   lightly crushed
1 teaspoon **chilli powder**
400 g (13 oz) **can chickpeas**,
   drained
2 x 400 g (13 oz) **cans peeled
   plum tomatoes**
2 tablespoons **black treacle**
1 tablespoon **wine vinegar**
salt and **pepper**
chopped **coriander** to garnish

Heat the oil in a frying pan on the hob and add the onion and celery. Fry gently for 5 minutes, then add the courgettes, peppers, garlic, oregano, cumin and chilli powder. Fry gently for a further 5 minutes. Turn into a casserole dish and stir in the chickpeas.

Tip the canned tomatoes into the frying pan and add the treacle and vinegar. Bring to the boil and add to the casserole dish, stirring the ingredients to combine. Place on the lower rack of the halogen oven.

Set the temperature to 200°C (392°F) and cook for 50 minutes until thick and pulpy. Season with salt and pepper, and serve in bowls over a bed of steamed rice. Top with spoonfuls of soured cream, if liked, and scatter with chopped coriander to garnish.

For mixed bean & butternut chilli, cut away the skin and discard the seeds from 1 small butternut squash, 750 g–1 kg (1½–2 lb). Cut the flesh into dice. Heat 2 tablespoons vegetable oil in a frying pan on the hob and fry the squash for 10 minutes until softened and beginning to brown. Drain to a plate while frying the vegetables and spices as above. Complete as above, replacing the chickpeas with a 400 g (13 oz) can mixed beans, drained, and adding the squash to the casserole halfway through cooking.

leek & chestnut parcels

Serves **8**
Preparation time **20 minutes**
Cooking time **20 minutes**

75 g (3 oz) **butter**
2 small **leeks**, trimmed and
    chopped
75 g (3 oz) **cooked chestnuts**,
    chopped
4 tablespoons **single cream**
2 tablespoons chopped
    parsley
freshly grated **nutmeg**
300 g (10 oz) **filo pastry**, cut
    into 24 x 12 cm (5 inch)
    squares
salt and **pepper**

Dressing
4 tablespoons **extra virgin
    olive oil**
1 tablespoon **white wine
    vinegar**
1 teaspoon **clear honey**
1 teaspoon **wholegrain
    mustard**

Melt 25 g (1 oz) of the butter in a frying pan on the hob
and gently fry the leeks until very soft. Leave to cool.
Add the chopped chestnuts, cream, parsley and plenty
of nutmeg. Season lightly with salt and pepper. Melt the
remaining butter in a small saucepan.

Brush 4 of the filo squares lightly with melted butter
and position a second square on top, adjusting the
angle to create a star shape. Brush lightly with more
butter and position a third layer, again adjusting the
angle. Divide half the filling equally among the centres.
Lift up the pastry edges and pinch together to parcels.
Repeat with the remainder of the pastry and filling, so
that you end up with 8 parcels, and place in a shallow
roasting tin. Brush with the remaining butter. Place on
the lower rack of the halogen oven.

Set the temperature to 200°C (392°F) and cook for
10–15 minutes until the pastry is golden and crisp.
While cooking, mix together the dressing ingredients in
a small bowl. Arrange the filo parcels on a bed of rocket
and drizzle with the dressing.

For Roquefort, walnut & pear parcels, melt the butter
in a frying pan as above and gently fry 50 g (2 oz)
walnut pieces and 2 peeled, cored and chopped pears
until softened. Leave to cool and stir in 75 g (3 oz)
crumbled Roquefort cheese. Season to taste with salt
and pepper, and use to fill the pastry squares. Cook and
serve as above.

warm asparagus & haloumi salad

Serves **6**
Preparation time **15 minutes**
Cooking time **about 15 minutes**

5 tablespoons **extra virgin olive oil**
1 tablespoon **lemon juice**
1 teaspoon **caster sugar**
1 tablespoon finely chopped **parsley**
400 g (13 oz) **haloumi cheese**, cut into thin slices
375 g (12 oz) **fresh asparagus**
2 tablespoons **capers**, rinsed and drained
salt and **pepper**

Mix together 4 tablespoons of the oil, the lemon juice, sugar and parsley in a small bowl. Season with salt and pepper. Set aside.

Pat the cheese slices dry on kitchen paper. Brush the asparagus with the remaining oil and a little seasoning. Place the asparagus on the upper rack of the halogen oven.

Set the temperature to 200°C (392°F) and cook for 5 minutes. Transfer to the lower rack to keep warm. Place the haloumi slices on the upper rack and cook for a couple of minutes on each side. (You will need to cook the cheese in batches.)

Arrange the asparagus and haloumi on serving plates and scatter with the capers. Lightly whisk the dressing and drizzle over the salad. Serve with lemon wedges and grainy bread.

For quick & easy hollandaise sauce to serve as an accompaniment, put 1 tablespoon white wine vinegar in a food processor with 3 egg yolks and a little salt and pepper. Melt 200 g (7 oz) unsalted butter in a small saucepan. With the food processor running, gradually pour the warm melted butter into the machine in a thin, steady stream so that the sauce gradually thickens. (Leave behind any sediments that collect in the bottom of the saucepan.) Season to taste with salt and pepper, adding a dash more vinegar if liked for extra tang, and serve spooned over the warm asparagus.

veggie breakfast sausages

Makes **12**
Preparation time **25 minutes,**
  plus cooling and chilling
Cooking time **25 minutes**

350 g (11½ oz) **carrots**, sliced
1 tablespoon **vegetable oil**,
  plus extra for oiling
1 **onion**, finely chopped
175 g (6 oz) **Cheddar**
  cheese, finely grated
225 g (7½ oz) **fresh white**
  breadcrumbs
3 tablespoons finely chopped
  parsley
2 tablespoons finely chopped
  sage
1 **egg**, beaten
1 **egg yolk**
plain flour, for dusting
salt and **pepper**

Cook the carrots in lightly salted boiling water for about 8 minutes until only just tender. Drain thoroughly and leave to cool. Process in a food processor until finely chopped.

Heat the oil in a frying pan on the hob and gently fry the onion for 2–3 minutes to soften. Tip into a bowl, add the carrots, Cheddar cheese, breadcrumbs, herbs, a little salt and plenty of pepper. Stir well to mix. Add the egg and yolk, and mix to a dough that holds together.

Turn out on to a lightly floured surface and divide into 12 even-sized portions. Shape each into a sausage and arrange on a lightly oiled baking sheet, spacing them slightly apart. Cover loosely and chill for 30 minutes. Place the baking sheet on the upper rack of the halogen oven.

Set the temperature to 225°C (437°F) and cook for 12–15 minutes, turning the sausages once they are golden on the surface and watching closely to check that they do not brown too much. Serve with fried mushrooms and baked beans.

For white bean & lovage sausages, thoroughly drain 2 x 400 g (13 oz) cans cannellini beans and blend in a food processor with 2 tablespoons chopped lovage, 2 tablespoons chopped parsley, 1 teaspoon ground coriander and a little salt and pepper. Fry 1 chopped onion in 1 tablespoon vegetable oil until softened. Mix in a bowl with the bean mixture, 100 g (3½ oz) fresh white breadcrumbs, 75 g (2 oz) grated Parmesan cheese and 1 beaten egg. Shape and cook as above.

142

Camembert-stuffed mushrooms

Serves **2**
Preparation time **15 minutes**
Cooking time **15 minutes**

2 **garlic cloves**, finely chopped
25 g (1 oz) **rocket**
100 ml (3½ fl oz) **extra virgin olive oil**
65 g (2½ oz) **fresh white breadcrumbs**
4 large **portobello mushrooms**, stalks removed
150 g (5 oz) **Camembert cheese**, cut into 8 slices
1 **beef tomato**, cut into 4 slices about 1 cm (½ inch) thick
salt and **pepper**

Put the garlic, rocket and 75 ml (3 fl oz) of the olive oil in a food processor and process to make a thick pesto-like paste. Season with salt and pepper, add 50 g (2 oz) of the breadcrumbs and process lightly to mix.

Arrange the mushrooms in a shallow roasting tin or on a baking sheet. Drizzle with the remaining oil and season with a little salt and pepper. Place on the upper rack of the halogen oven.

Set the temperature to 200°C (392°F) and cook for 5 minutes. Place a slice of Camembert on each mushroom. Top each with a tomato slice, then the remaining Camembert. Spoon the rocket paste on top and scatter with the remaining breadcrumbs.

Place on the lower rack of the halogen oven and cook for 5–10 minutes until the breadcrumbs are golden. Serve with grainy bread and a leafy salad or pak choi.

For braised pak choi to serve as an accompaniment, halve 3 pak choi lengthways and cook in boiling water for 2 minutes. Drain thoroughly and place in a shallow ovenproof dish. In a frying pan, gently fry ½ bunch of chopped spring onions, 1 sliced garlic clove and 1 cored, deseeded and diced red pepper in 1 tablespoon wok or vegetable oil. Scatter over the pak choi. Mix together 150 ml (¼ pint) coconut cream, 1 tablespoon clear honey, 1 tablespoon rice vinegar and 3 tablespoons chopped coriander in a small bowl. Pour over the pak choi. Heat 2 tablespoons sesame oil in the pan and stir in 40 g (1½ oz) fresh, white breadcrumbs. Scatter into the dish and cook on the upper rack of the halogen oven at 200°C (392°F).

cherry tomato & pepper tart

Serves **4**
Preparation time **10 minutes**
Cooking time **20 minutes**

375 g (12 oz) **ready-prepared puff pastry**
plain flour, **for dusting**
vegetable oil, **for oiling**
4 tablespoons **red pesto**
200 g (7 oz) **cherry tomatoes**, halved
150 g (5 oz) **mixed roasted peppers**, roughly chopped
100 g (3½ oz) **feta cheese**, crumbled
salt and **pepper**
basil leaves, to garnish

Roll out the pastry thinly on a lightly floured surface and cut out a 25 cm (10 inch) round. Place on a lightly oiled baking sheet. Using the tip of a sharp knife, make a shallow cut 1 cm (½ inch) away from the edge of the pastry to form a border. Place on the upper rack of the halogen oven.

Set the temperature to 250°C (482°F) and cook the pastry case for 12 minutes, lifting out the risen centre in a layer from the pastry case towards the end of the cooking time.

Meanwhile mix the pesto in a bowl with the tomatoes, peppers and feta. Spread in an even layer over the pastry, making sure that the filling is contained within the scored rim. Season with salt and pepper. Return to the upper rack of the halogen oven.

Reduce the temperature to 225°C (437°F) and cook for a further 10 minutes until the pastry is puffed and golden, covering with foil if the pastry starts to brown too much. Serve scattered with basil leaves to garnish.

For veggie pissaladière, fry 3 large sliced onions in 4 tablespoons olive oil on the hob for about 15 minutes until very soft but not browned. Season with salt and pepper. Stir in 1 tablespoon chopped lemon thyme. Bake the pastry case as above and spread the onion mixture over the centre. Scatter with 10 pitted black olives and 2 teaspoons rinsed and drained capers. Season lightly with salt and pepper, and cook as above.

cauliflower & potato curry

Serves **4**
Preparation time **20 minutes**
Cooking time **1 hour**

500 g (1 lb) small **potatoes**,
    quartered
3 tablespoons **vegetable oil**
1 small **cauliflower**, about
    625 g (1¼ lb), cut into
    florets
1 **onion**, sliced
2 **garlic cloves**, crushed
2 teaspoons **garam masala**
2 teaspoons **ground cumin**
½ teaspoon **ground turmeric**
½ teaspoon **hot chilli powder**
150 ml (¼ pint) **vegetable
    stock**
4 **tomatoes**, skinned and
    chopped
salt

Cook the potatoes in a saucepan of salted boiling
water on the hob for 6–8 minutes until softened. Drain
and transfer to a casserole dish.

Heat 2 tablespoons of the oil in a frying pan and fry the
cauliflower and onion for 5 minutes until beginning to
colour. Add to the casserole dish. Heat the remaining
oil in the frying pan and add the garlic and spices.
Heat gently for 30 seconds, then stir in the stock and
tomatoes. Bring to the boil and add to the casserole
dish. Cover with foil and place on the lower rack of the
halogen oven.

Set the temperature to 200°C (392°F) and cook for
about 45 minutes until the vegetables are tender.
Check the seasoning, adding salt if needed, and serve
with pilau rice.

For pilau rice with almonds to serve as an
accompaniment, heat 3 tablespoons vegetable oil in
a large frying pan and gently fry 50 g (2 oz) flaked
almonds until lightly browned. Drain the almonds with
a slotted spoon and set aside. Add 1 chopped onion
to the pan and fry gently for 5 minutes. Add 2 crushed
garlic cloves, a 4 cm (1¾ inch) piece of fresh root
ginger, chopped, and 225 g (7½ oz) basmati rice. Cook
for 1 minute. Add 300 ml (½ pint) vegetable stock,
½ teaspoon crumbled saffron threads, 50 g (2 oz)
raisins and a little salt and pepper. Bring to the boil,
reduce the heat and simmer gently for about 20
minutes until the rice is tender, adding a dash more
stock if the pilau dries out before the rice is cooked.
To serve, season to taste and stir in the almonds and
3 tablespoons chopped parsley.

pizza & pasta

tuna rigatoni bake

Serves **4**
Preparation time **15 minutes**
Cooking time **35 minutes**

200 g (7 oz) **dried rigatoni**
2 tablespoons **olive oil**
2 **courgettes**, thinly sliced
200 g (7 oz) **can tuna**, drained
225 g (7½ oz) **cottage cheese**
400 g (13 oz) **can chopped tomatoes**
2 tablespoons **sun-dried tomato paste**
1 teaspoon **caster sugar**
75 g (3 oz) **fontina** or **Cheddar cheese**, grated
salt and **pepper**

Cook the pasta in salted boiling water for about 8 minutes until just tender. Drain. While the pasta is cooking, heat the oil in a frying pan on the hob and gently fry the courgettes for about 5 minutes, turning frequently, until they colour.

Flake the tuna into chunky pieces and mix with the cottage cheese in a bowl. In a separate bowl, mix the tomatoes with the tomato paste, sugar, salt and pepper.

Scatter half the pasta over the bottom of a shallow ovenproof dish and arrange a layer of half the tuna mixture, then a layer of half the courgettes on top. Spoon over half the tomatoes. Repeat the layering with the remaining ingredients, finishing with tomatoes.

Sprinkle with the cheese and cover with foil. Place on the lower rack of the halogen oven.

Set the temperature to 200°C (392°F) and cook for 15 minutes. Remove the foil and cook for another 5–10 minutes until lightly browned. Serve with a leafy salad.

For spicy sausage bake, cook 200 g (7 oz) dried rigatoni as above. Line the upper rack of the halogen oven with foil and arrange 450 g (14½ oz) Italian sausages, side by side, on top. Scatter with 1 chopped onion and drizzle with 1 tablespoon olive oil. Grill at 200°C (392°F) for about 20 minutes until the sausages are cooked. Slice the sausages and toss with the onion, pasta, 2 x 400 g (13 oz) cans chopped tomatoes, 1 teaspoon caster sugar, 1 tablespoon chopped oregano, 1 tablespoon hot chilli sauce and 75 g (3 oz) grated Cheddar cheese. Turn into an ovenproof dish and sprinkle with 50 g (2 oz) grated Cheddar. Cook as above.

chorizo & olive linguine

Serves **2**
Preparation time **10 minutes**
Cooking time **15 minutes**

75 g (3 oz) **cooking chorizo
  sausage**, skinned and diced
2 tablespoons **olive oil**
1 **garlic clove**, crushed
100 g (3½ oz) **canned butter
  beans**, drained
75 g (3 oz) **pitted black
  olives**, roughly chopped
1 teaspoon **Tabasco sauce**
12 **cherry tomatoes**, halved
125 g (4 oz) **dried linguine**
3 tablespoons chopped
  parsley
50 g (2 oz) **Manchego
  cheese**, shaved
salt

Put the chorizo and olive oil in a small roasting tin and place on the upper rack of the halogen oven. Set the temperature to 200°C (392°F) and cook for 5 minutes, stirring once. Add the garlic, beans, olives, Tabasco sauce, cherry tomatoes and a little salt. Cook for a further 3–4 minutes until hot.

Meanwhile, cook the pasta in plenty of salted boiling water for about 6 minutes until just tender. Drain well and return to the pan. Stir in the chorizo mixture and then tip into a shallow ovenproof dish, adding the parsley and Manchego.

Place on the upper rack of the halogen oven and set the temperature to 150°C (302°F). Cook for 5 minutes until heated through.

For linguine primavera, thinly slice a large fennel bulb and put in a shallow roasting tin with 25 g (1 oz) butter. Place on the upper rack of the halogen oven and set the temperature to 200°C (392°F). Cook for 5 minutes, stirring once. Cook 75 g (3 oz) baby carrots in salted boiling water until almost tender. Add 50 g (2 oz) podded fresh or frozen broad beans and 50 g (2 oz) peas and cook for a further 2 minutes. Tip in 100 g (3½ oz) fresh asparagus tips and cook for a further 1 minute. Drain well. Cook 125 g (4 oz) dried linguine as above, drain and toss in a shallow dish with the fennel and other vegetables. Drizzle with 150 ml (¼ pint) double cream, sprinkle with grated Parmesan cheese and season with salt and pepper. Gently heat through as above.

154

spaghetti carbonara

Serves **2**
Preparation time **5 minutes**
Cooking time **about 10
   minutes**

50 g (2 oz) **pancetta** or
   streaky bacon, finely
   chopped
1 tablespoon **olive oil**
2 **egg yolks**
25 g (1 oz) **Parmesan
   cheese**, grated, plus extra
   to serve
75 ml (3 fl oz) **single cream**
200 g (7 oz) **fresh spaghetti**
salt and **pepper**
snipped **chives**, to garnish

Put the pancetta or bacon and the olive oil in a small
roasting tin and place on the upper rack of the halogen
oven. Set the temperature to 200°C (392°F) and cook
for 4–5 minutes, stirring once, until browned.

Mix together the egg yolks, Parmesan and cream in a
bowl. Season to taste.

Cook the pasta in plenty of salted boiling water for
2–3 minutes until tender. Drain and turn into a shallow
ovenproof dish. Add the cream and egg mixture and tip
in the cooked pancetta or bacon. Stir lightly and cover
with foil.

Place on the upper rack of the halogen oven and
set the temperature to 175°C (347°F). Cook for
2–3 minutes until hot and the cream and egg mixture
is lightly cooked. Serve sprinkled with extra grated or
shaved Parmesan garnished with snipped chives.

For spaghetti with roasted tomato sauce, arrange
600 g (1 lb 2 oz) halved ripe tomatoes, cut sides facing
up, in a single layer in a shallow ovenproof dish and
sprinkle with 2 finely chopped shallots, 1 teaspoon dried
oregano, 1 tablespoon olive oil, 1 teaspoon caster sugar
and a little salt and pepper. Place on the lower rack of
the halogen oven and set the temperature to 225°C
(437°F). Cook for about 30 minutes until the tomatoes
are lightly browned. Heat 3 tablespoons olive oil in a
saucepan on the hob and fry 2 teaspoons crushed
coriander seeds for 1 minute until fragrant. Stir in the
roasted tomato mixture and mix well. Blend in a food
processor until smooth. Cook the spaghetti as above
and serve with the roasted tomato sauce.

156

spinach & ricotta cannelloni

Serves **4**

Preparation time **30 minutes**

Cooking time **35 minutes**

6–8 **dried cannelloni tubes**

300 g (10 oz) **fresh spinach**

1 tablespoon **water**

75 g (3 oz) **Parma ham**,
  chopped

200 g (7 oz) **ricotta cheese**

freshly grated **nutmeg**

350 g (11½ oz) tub **ready-
  made béchamel sauce**

50 g (2 oz) **Parmesan
  cheese**, grated

15 g (½ oz) **dried
  breadcrumbs**

salt and **pepper**

Cook the pasta in plenty of salted boiling water for 8–10 minutes until just tender. Drain.

Pack the spinach into a saucepan and drizzle with the measurement water. Cover and cook for 2–3 minutes until wilted. Drain thoroughly and turn into a bowl. Add the Parma ham, ricotta and plenty of nutmeg. Season with salt and pepper, and mix well.

Spoon the mixture into the pasta tubes, taking care not to tear them, and arrange side by side in a shallow ovenproof dish. Spoon the sauce over the pasta and sprinkle with the Parmesan and breadcrumbs. Place on the upper rack of the halogen oven.

Set the temperature to 200°C (392°F) and cook for 15–20 minutes until the cheese is melting and lightly browned.

For cannelloni with salmon & dill, cook 12 cannelloni tubes as above and drain. Put 300 g (10 oz) lightly smoked salmon in a frying pan on the hob with 3 tablespoons milk. Cover and poach for 6–8 minutes until just cooked. Drain and flake the fish. Cook 250 g (8 oz) frozen peas and crush lightly. Mix with the salmon, plenty of pepper and 3 tablespoons ready-made béchamel sauce taken from a 350 g (11½ oz) tub. Pack into the cannelloni and arrange in a shallow ovenproof dish as above. Stir 4 tablespoons chopped dill into the remaining béchamel sauce and spoon over the pasta. Sprinkle with 50 g (2 oz) grated Gruyère cheese and cook as above.

pasta, red onion & beetroot gratin

Serves **4**
Preparation time **20 minutes**
Cooking time **30 minutes**

250 g (8 oz) **dried penne**
2 tablespoons **olive oil**
3 large **red onions,**
  thinly sliced
1 tablespoon chopped **thyme,**
  plus extra to garnish
2 **garlic cloves,** crushed
350 g (11½ oz) tub **ready-**
  made béchamel sauce
75 g (3 oz) **Emmental** or
  Gruyère cheese, grated
275 g (9 oz) **cooked**
  beetroot, sliced
salt and **pepper**

Cook the pasta in plenty of salted boiling water for about 10 minutes until just tender. Drain and return to the pan.

Meanwhile heat the oil in a large frying pan on the hob and gently fry the onions for about 10 minutes, stirring frequently, until beginning to brown. Add the thyme and garlic, and fry for a further 1 minute. Add to the drained pasta along with half the béchamel sauce and cheese.

Turn half the mixture into a shallow ovenproof dish and scatter the beetroot slices on top. Tip the remaining pasta over the beetroot and spoon over the remaining sauce. Sprinkle with the remaining cheese and place on the upper rack of the halogen oven.

Set the temperature to 200°C (392°F) and cook for 15–20 minutes until the sauce is bubbling and turning golden. Serve garnished with thyme.

For pasta verde with artichokes, cook 250 g (8 oz) tagliatelle verde in salted boiling water for about 8 minutes until just tender. Drain a 275 g (9 oz) jar artichokes in olive oil, reserving the oil, and slice the artichokes if not already sliced. Heat 3 tablespoons of the reserved oil in a frying pan and gently fry 2 sliced onions and 1 sliced fennel bulb for about 10 minutes until very soft. Stir in 2 tablespoons rinsed and drained capers. Combine the pasta, a 350 g (11½ oz) tub ready-made béchamel sauce and 75 g (3 oz) grated Emmental or Gruyère cheese as above and layer up in a shallow ovenproof dish with the artichokes before cooking in the halogen oven.

penne with asparagus & pastrami

Serves **4**

Preparation time **10 minutes**

Cooking time **15 minutes**

300 g (10 oz) **dried penne**

250 g (9 oz) **fresh asparagus tips**

15 g (½ oz) **butter**

100 g (3½ oz) **sun-dried tomatoes in olive oil**, drained and thinly sliced, plus 3 tablespoons of the oil

200 g (7 oz) **pastrami**, chopped

2 teaspoons **lemon juice**

salt and **pepper**

Parmesan cheese shavings, to serve

Cook the pasta in plenty of salted boiling water for about 10 minutes until just tender. Drain and return to the pan.

Meanwhile, scatter the asparagus in a shallow roasting tin. Dot with the butter and season lightly. Place on the upper rack of the halogen oven.

Set the temperature to 250°C (482°F) and cook the asparagus for about 5 minutes until just tender. (The time will depend on the thickness of the spears.)

Put the asparagus, sun-dried tomatoes, the 3 tablespoons olive oil and pastrami in the pan with the pasta. Sprinkle over the lemon juice and season with salt and pepper. Mix well and turn into a shallow ovenproof dish. Place on the lower rack of the halogen oven.

Set the temperature to 200°C (392°F) and cook for 5 minutes to heat through. Serve scattered with Parmesan shavings.

For gnocchi with broad beans & pancetta, cook 500 g (1 lb) gnocchi in a large saucepan of salted boiling water for 3 minutes or until it rises to the surface. Transfer the gnocchi with a slotted spoon to an ovenproof dish. Cook 200 g (7 oz) fresh broad beans in the pan until just tender and scatter over the gnocchi. Melt 75 g (3 oz) butter in a small frying pan and gently fry 100 g (3½ oz) chopped pancetta until golden. Scatter the pancetta over the gnocchi and drizzle with the excess butter. Grate 100 g (3½ oz) mature Cheddar cheese. Cook on the lower rack of the halogen oven for about 15 minutes until cheese is melted and bubbling.

spaghetti with prawns & chilli

Serves **4**

Preparation time **15 minutes**

Cooking time **15 minutes**

450 g (14½ oz) small **ripe tomatoes**, skinned

3 tablespoons **olive oil**

1 bunch of **spring onions**, sliced

4 **garlic cloves**, crushed

1 medium **fresh red chilli**, deseeded and chopped

300 g (10 oz) **fresh spaghetti**

400 g (13 oz) **raw** peeled and deveined **king prawns**

salt

Halve the tomatoes and scoop out the seeds. Roughly chop the flesh. Set aside.

Put 2 tablespoons of the olive oil in a shallow roasting tin with the spring onions, garlic and chilli. Place on the upper rack of the halogen oven.

Set the temperature to 225°C/437°F and cook for 2 minutes. Add the chopped tomatoes and a little salt and cook for a further 2 minutes.

Cook the pasta in a saucepan of salted boiling water for 2 minutes or until just tender. Drain well, return to the pan and stir in the tomato mixture. Tip into a shallow ovenproof dish and scatter with the prawns.

Brush the prawns with the remaining oil and place the tin on the lower rack of the halogen oven.

Set the temperature to 250°C (482°F) and cook for about 8 minutes until the prawns have turned pink and are just cooked through, turning them once halfway through cooking.

For macaroni chilli cheese, cook 250 g (8 oz) macaroni in plenty of salted boiling water for 8–10 minutes until just tender. Drain and return to the pan. Stir in a 350 g (11½ oz) tub ready-made béchamel sauce, 100 g (3½ oz) grated mature Cheddar cheese, 1 chopped bunch of spring onions, 1 deseeded and chopped medium fresh red chilli and 4 tablespoons chopped coriander. Turn into a shallow ovenproof dish and sprinkle with a little extra Cheddar. Place on the lower rack of the halogen oven and cook at 200°C (392°F) for 15–20 minutes until golden.

goats' cheese & mushroom pizza

Serves **2**
Preparation time **10 minutes**
Cooking time **8 minutes**

1 **ready-made thin and crispy
   pizza base**
2 tablespoons **onion relish**
2 **tomatoes**, thinly sliced
50 g (2 oz) **button
   mushrooms**, thinly sliced
150 g (5 oz) **goats' cheese
   with rind**, thinly sliced
2 tablespoons **extra virgin
   olive oil**
2 tablespoons **basil pesto**
salt and **pepper**
rocket, to garnish

Remove the lower rack from the halogen oven and place the pizza base on top.

Spread the pizza base with the onion relish. Scatter the tomatoes and mushrooms over the relish. Arrange the slices of goats' cheese on top. Sprinkle with salt and pepper, drizzle with 1 tablespoon of the oil and position the rack in the oven.

Set the temperature to 200°C (392°F) and cook the pizza for about 8 minutes until the cheese is melting. While cooking, blend the pesto with the remaining olive oil.

Drizzle the cooked pizza with the pesto mixture and scatter with rocket to garnish. Cut the pizza into slices and serve.

For wild mushroom & mozzarella pizza, scatter 1 thinly sliced onion over the bottom of a shallow roasting tin and drizzle with 2 tablespoons olive oil. Place on the upper rack of the halogen oven and set the temperature to 200°C (392°F). Cook for 5 minutes. Toss the onion with 1 chopped garlic clove, 200 g (7 oz) sliced mixed wild mushrooms and 2 tablespoons truffle oil. Scatter over 1 ready-made thin and crispy pizza base and arrange 150 g (5 oz) sliced mozzarella cheese on top. Season lightly with salt and pepper, and bake as above. Serve sprinkled with chopped parsley.

easy pepperoni pizza

Serves **2**
Preparation time **5 minutes**
Cooking time **8 minutes**

2 **plain naan breads**
200 g (7 oz) **ready-made tomato sauce for pasta**
100 g (3½ oz) **cherry tomatoes**, halved
150 g (5 oz) **mozzarella cheese**, thinly sliced
50 g (2 oz) **pepperoni**, thinly sliced
1 tablespoon **olive oil**
salt and **pepper**
handful of **basil** leaves

Lay the naan breads, side by side, in a shallow roasting tin and spread with the tomato sauce.

Scatter with the tomatoes, mozzarella slices and pepperoni. Drizzle with the oil and season lightly with salt and pepper. Place on the upper rack of the halogen oven.

Set the temperature to 200°C (392°F) and cook for 6–8 minutes until the cheese is melting. Serve scattered with basil leaves.

For easy Sicilian pizzas, place the naan breads in a shallow roasting tin as above and spread with the tomato sauce. Drain 4 canned anchovy fillets and slice in half lengthways. Sprinkle the tomato sauce with 75 g (3 oz) grated Grana Padano or pecorino cheese. Arrange the anchovies on top and scatter with 2 teaspoons rinsed and drained capers. Cook as above.

crostini with peppers

Serves **2–4**
Preparation time **5 minutes**
Cooking time **8 minutes**

4 slices of **rustic Italian bread** such as **ciabatta**
1 **garlic clove**, halved
2 tablespoons finely chopped **parsley**
2 tablespoons **extra virgin olive oil**, plus extra to serve
175 g (6 oz) **roasted mixed peppers**, cut into strips
4 tablespoons **black olive tapenade**
salt and **pepper**
roughly chopped **parsley**, to garnish

Put the bread slices on the upper rack of the halogen oven. Set the temperature to 250°C (482°F) and cook the bread for 1–2 minutes on each side until toasted and lightly golden.

Rub the cut sides of the garlic clove over one side of each slice of toast and sprinkle with the parsley.

Drizzle with the olive oil and pile the peppers on top. Return to the upper rack of the oven. Set the temperature to 175°C (347°F) and cook for 3–4 minutes until heated through. Transfer to serving plates and place spoonfuls of tapenade on each crostini. Scatter with chopped parsley and serve drizzled with extra olive oil.

For homemade black olive tapenade, put 150 g (5 oz) pitted black olives, 2 tablespoons rinsed and drained capers, ½ x 50 g (2 oz) can anchovies, drained, and 2 garlic cloves in a food processor. Process to a paste. Add a small handful of chopped parsley, a squeeze of lemon juice, 100 ml (3½ fl oz) olive oil and plenty of pepper. Process until evenly mixed, then transfer to a bowl or jar. Cover and store in the refrigerator for up to 3 weeks.

gorgonzola & rocket pizza

Serves **2**

Preparation time **25 minutes, plus proving**

Cooking time **35 minutes**

250 g (8 oz) **strong white flour**, plus extra for dusting

2½ teaspoons **easy-blend dried yeast**

1 teaspoon **salt**

3 tablespoons **olive oil**, plus extra for oiling

125 ml (4 fl oz) hand-hot **water**

Topping

2 tablespoons **olive oil**

1 **onion**, chopped

2 **garlic cloves**, crushed

400 g (13 oz) **can chopped tomatoes**

2 tablespoons **sun-dried tomato paste**

2 tablespoons **basil pesto**

1 teaspoon **mixed dried herbs**

250 g (8 oz) **Gorgonzola cheese**

handful of **rocket**

balsamic vinegar

salt and **pepper**

Put the flour, yeast, salt and oil in a bowl and add the measurement water. Mix with a round-bladed knife to a dough, adding a dash more water if the mixture feels dry. Turn out onto a lightly floured surface and knead for about 10 minutes until smooth and elastic. Place in a lightly oiled bowl, cover with clingfilm and leave to rise in a warm place for about 1 hour until doubled in size.

Heat the oil in a frying pan on the hob and gently fry the onion for 5 minutes. Stir in the garlic, tomatoes, tomato paste, pesto and herbs, and season with salt and pepper. Cook for 15 minutes until thickened.

Oil a pizza tray lightly. Tip the dough out on to a lightly floured surface and roll out into a round slightly smaller than the tray. Transfer to the tray and spread with the tomato sauce. Crumble the Gorgonzola over the sauce. Place the tray on the upper rack of the halogen oven.

Set the temperature to 200°C (392°F) and cook for 15 minutes. Serve the pizza cut into slices, scattered with the rocket and drizzled with balsamic vinegar.

For goats' cheese & red onion pizza, make the pizza dough as above. Scatter 2 sliced red onions in the bottom of a shallow roasting tin and drizzle with 3 tablespoons olive oil. Place on the upper rack of the halogen oven and set the temperature to 200°C (392°F). Cook for 6–8 minutes, stirring once, until the onions are soft. Stir in 1 teaspoon chopped rosemary. Roll out the dough as above and scatter with the onions, 200 g (7 oz) sliced goats' cheese and 50 g (2 oz) grated Parmesan cheese. Season lightly and cook as above.

on the side

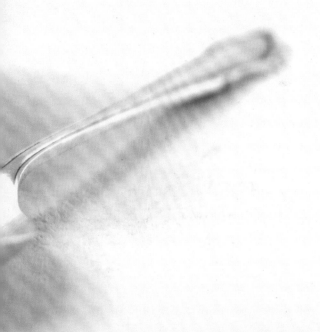

caramel roasted vegetables

Serves **4**
Preparation time **15 minutes**
Cooking time **30 minutes**

2 tablespoons **olive oil**
4 cm (1¾ inch) piece of **fresh
    root ginger**, sliced
40 g (1½ oz) **dark
    muscovado sugar**
3 tablespoons **dark soy sauce**
juice of 1 **lime**
1 small **butternut squash**,
    about 625 g (1¼ lb) peeled,
    deseeded and cut into 2.5
    cm (1 inch) cubes
2 small **sweet potatoes**, cut
    into 2.5 cm (1 inch) cubes
1 **aubergine**, cut into 2.5 cm
    (1 inch) cubes
2 **parsnips**, cut into wedges
2 **carrots**, cut into wedges
2 small **red onions**,
    thinly sliced
2 **garlic cloves**, thinly sliced

Mix together the olive oil, ginger, sugar, soy sauce and lime juice in a bowl. Add the vegetables, including the onions, and turn in the dressing until evenly coated. Scatter into a shallow roasting tin or ovenproof dish. Place on the lower rack of the halogen oven.

Set the temperature to 250°C (482°F) and cook for 15 minutes. Add the garlic and toss the vegetables together. Cook for a further 15 minutes or until caramelized. Serve with roast or grilled chicken, pork or duck.

For spiced yogurt sauce to serve as an accompaniment, put 2 trimmed and sliced spring onions, 1 chopped garlic clove, a handful of chopped coriander, 1 deseeded and finely chopped fresh red chilli and a little salt in a food processor with 150 ml (¼ pint) Greek yogurt. Process until evenly mixed. Turn into a bowl and stir in 4 tablespoons crème fraîche. Spoon into a small serving dish, cover and chill until ready to serve.

aubergines with harissa dressing

Serves **6**
Preparation time **15 minutes, plus standing**
Cooking time **25 minutes**

3 small **aubergines**, cut lengthways into thin slices
2 **garlic cloves**, roughly chopped
1 teaspoon **harissa paste**
2 teaspoons **ground cumin**
2 teaspoons **ground coriander**
1 teaspoon **paprika**
1 tablespoon **lemon juice**
15 g (½ oz) **fresh coriander**
5 g (¼ oz) **mint**
125 ml (4 fl oz) **extra virgin olive oil**
salt
chopped **parsley**, to garnish

Layer the aubergine slices in a colander, sprinkling each layer with salt. Leave to stand for 30 minutes. Rinse thoroughly to remove all the salt and pat dry on kitchen paper.

Process the garlic, harissa paste, ground spices, lemon juice, coriander, mint and 75 ml (3 fl oz) of the olive oil in a food processor to make a thin paste.

Brush the upper rack of the halogen oven lightly with some of the remaining oil and lay the aubergine slices on it. (You will need to cook the aubergines in several batches.) Brush with more oil and cook for 5–6 minutes, turning once and brushing with more oil, until tender. Keep warm while cooking the remainder.

Arrange on a serving plate, drizzle with the sauce and garnish with chopped parsley.

For caponata, cut 3 small aubergines widthways into slices and grill as above. Heat 2 tablespoons olive oil in a large saucepan and fry 1 finely chopped onion for 5 minutes. Add the aubergines, 800 g (1 lb 10 oz) canned chopped tomatoes, 1 tablespoon red wine vinegar, 2 teaspoons light muscovado sugar, 2 tablespoons rinsed and drained capers, 50 g (2 oz) pitted and chopped black olives and a handful of chopped parsley. Cook gently for about 15 minutes until thick and pulpy. Serve warm or cold.

garlicky potato bake

Serves **6**
Preparation time **20 minutes**
Cooking time **1¼ hours**

25 g (1 oz) **butter**, plus extra
   for greasing
1 tablespoon **vegetable oil**
2 **onions**, sliced
3 **garlic cloves**, crushed
1 kg (2 lb) waxy **potatoes**, very
   thinly sliced
about 450 ml (¾ pint) hot
   chicken stock
salt and **pepper**

Melt the butter with the oil in a frying pan on the hob
and fry the onions for 5 minutes. Stir in the garlic and
fry for a further 2 minutes.

Layer up half the potatoes in a lightly greased
ovenproof dish and scatter with the onions. Layer
the remaining potatoes on top and season with salt
and pepper.

Pour over the stock until it only just reaches the top
layer of potatoes. Cover the dish with foil and place on
the lower rack of the halogen oven.

Set the temperature to 250°C (482°F) and cook for
50 minutes or until the potatoes are cooked through.
Remove the foil and bake for a further 15 minutes or
until the potatoes are golden. Serve with roast beef,
lamb or steak.

For dauphinoise potatoes, fry the onions and garlic
and layer up with the potatoes in an ovenproof dish
as above, scattering the onions with 2 tablespoons
chopped rosemary. Gently heat 450 ml (¾ pint) single
cream in a saucepan with a little salt and pepper, and
pour over the potatoes. Sprinkle the surface with a little
grated Parmesan cheese and bake as above.

root vegetable gratin

Serves **8**
Preparation time **25 minutes**
Cooking time **1½ hours**

125 g (4 oz) **butter**
3 **garlic cloves**, crushed
2 tablespoons chopped **thyme**
freshly grated **nutmeg**
750 g (1½ lb) **potatoes**,
   such as Maris Piper
450 g (14 ½ oz) **carrots**
400 g (13 oz) **celeriac**
300 g (10 oz) **swede**
100 ml (3½ fl oz) hot
   vegetable or **chicken stock**
salt and **pepper**

Melt the butter in a small saucepan and stir in the garlic, thyme and plenty of nutmeg. Season with salt and pepper.

Slice the potatoes, carrots, celeriac and swede as thinly as possible. (A food processor with a slicer attachment or a mandoline is ideal). Layer all the vegetables in an ovenproof dish, drizzling over a little of the flavoured butter as you assemble the dish.

Pour over the hot stock and cover the dish with foil. Place on the lower rack of the halogen oven.

Set the temperature to 250°C (482°F) and cook for 1–1¼ hours until the vegetables feel tender when pierced with a knife. Remove the foil and bake for a further 15 minutes or until the surface is golden. Serve with roast meats or poultry.

For crispy baked champ, cook 1 kg (2 lb) floury potatoes in salted boiling water until tender. Drain and return to the pan. Finely chop 1 bunch of spring onions and put in a small saucepan with 200 ml (7 fl oz) milk. Bring almost to the boil and leave to stand for 5 minutes. Add to the potatoes along with 50 g (2 oz) butter and mash until smooth. Turn into an ovenproof dish, sprinkle with 50 g (2 oz) finely grated Cheddar cheese and dot with extra butter. Cook, uncovered, on the lower rack of the halogen oven for 15 minutes or until golden.

spicy sweet potatoes

Serves **4**

Preparation time **10 minutes**

Cooking time **about 25 minutes**

10 **cardamom pods**

2 large **sweet potatoes**, about 250 g (8 oz) each, cut into thick slices

3 tablespoons **garlic- and herb-infused olive oil**

½ teaspoon **coriander seeds**, crushed

½ teaspoon **cumin seeds**, crushed

salt and **pepper**

Crush the cardamom pods using a mortar and pestle. Remove the husks and crush the seeds a little further.

Cook the sweet potatoes in salted boiling water for 5 minutes until softened but not falling apart. Drain well.

Mix together the olive oil, crushed spices and a little salt and pepper. Drizzle over the potatoes and turn them until coated. Arrange the sweet potatoes in a single layer on the upper rack of the halogen oven. (You will need to cook the sweet potatoes in batches.)

Set the temperature to 250°C (482°F) and cook for 3–5 minutes on each side until golden. Keep warm while cooking the remainder. Serve as a snack with a spicy or soured cream and chive dip, or to accompany roast pork or chicken.

For homemade garlic- and herb-infused olive oil, squash 3 garlic cloves with the back of a knife. Bruise a handful of fresh herbs such as basil, thyme, rosemary, fennel and parsley by squeezing them firmly in your hands. Put the herbs and garlic in a thoroughly clean glass bottle with a tight-fitting seal and top up with 300 ml (½ pint) olive oil. Store in the refrigerator and use within 3–4 weeks.

roasted beetroot couscous

Serves **6**
Preparation time **10 minutes**
Cooking time **45 minutes**

750 g (1½ lb) small fresh
  beetroot, cut into
  small wedges
75 ml (3 fl oz) **olive oil**
3 tablespoons **balsamic
  vinegar**
1 teaspoon **rosewater**
2 **garlic cloves**, finely chopped
4 tablespoons chopped
  chives
2 tablespoons chopped
  lovage, **savory** or **parsley**
275 g (9 oz) **instant couscous**
400 ml (14 fl oz) hot
  vegetable stock
50 g (2 oz) toasted **pine nuts**
salt and **pepper**

Scatter the beetroot wedges in a shallow roasting tin.
Drizzle with 1 tablespoon of the oil and a little salt and
pepper. Cover with foil and place on the upper rack of
the halogen oven.

Set the temperature to 250°C (482°F) and cook for
about 45 minutes, uncovering for the final 10 minutes,
until the beetroot is tender. While cooking, mix the
remaining oil with the vinegar, rosewater, garlic and
chopped herbs. Season with salt and pepper. Put the
couscous in a heatproof bowl, add the hot stock and
cover with foil. Leave to stand for 10 minutes until the
couscous has absorbed the stock.

Fluff up the couscous grains with a fork and stir in the
dressing and pine nuts until evenly mixed. Lightly stir in
the beetroot. Serve with roast duck or chicken.

For warm tabbouleh with apricots, cut 300 g
(10 oz) fresh apricots into wedges and scatter in a
shallow dish. Drizzle with 2 tablespoons lemon-infused
oil and place on the upper rack of the halogen oven.
Set the temperature to 200°C (392°F) and cook for
10 minutes, turning once or twice. Put 250 g (8 oz)
instant couscous in a heatproof bowl, cover with 350 ml
(12 fl oz) hot vegetable or chicken stock and leave to
stand for 10 minutes. Fluff up the couscous grains with
a fork and stir in 75 g (3 oz) chopped pistachio nuts,
1 small finely chopped red onion, 2 chopped garlic
cloves, a handful each of chopped mint and parsley,
the grated rind and juice of 1 lemon and 4 tablespoons
extra virgin olive oil. Season to taste with salt and
pepper. Lightly stir in the apricots to serve.

aubergine & mozzarella stacks

Serves **4**
Preparation time **30 minutes,
    plus standing and cooling**
Cooking time **25 minutes**

4 **garlic cloves**, peeled
1 large **aubergine**
4 tablespoons **olive oil**
5 **ripe tomatoes**, skinned,
    deseeded and diced
12 **sun-dried tomatoes in oil**,
    drained and finely chopped
4 tablespoons **sun-dried
    tomato paste**
handful of **basil leaves**,
    roughly chopped
6 tablespoons **basil pesto**
150 g (5 oz) **buffalo
    mozzarella cheese**, drained
    and cut into 4 pieces
balsamic vinegar, for drizzling
salt and **pepper**
rocket or **basil leaves**, to
    garnish

Put the garlic cloves on a sheet of foil and place on the upper rack of the halogen oven. Set the temperature to 250°C (482°F) and cook for 5–10 minutes until the garlic is soft. Be careful not to let it burn.

Cut the aubergine into 12 slices each about 1 cm (½ inch) thick. Layer the slices in a colander, sprinkling each layer with salt. Leave to stand for 30 minutes. Rinse thoroughly to remove all the salt and pat dry on kitchen paper. Brush the slices with the oil. Fry in a large frying pan on the hob, turning the slices once, for about 5 minutes until golden on both sides. Leave to cool.

Meanwhile, mash the softened garlic against the sides of a bowl. Stir in the diced tomatoes, sun-dried tomatoes, tomato paste and basil. Season to taste.

Make the stacks. Arrange 4 aubergine slices side-by-side in a shallow roasting tin and spread each one with a little pesto. Spoon a little of the tomato mixture on top, then place another aubergine slice on top of that. Spoon over a little more tomato mixture, then add another slice of aubergine. Spread with the remaining pesto. Place a piece of mozzarella on top of each stack, securing in place by pushing a skewer down through the centre of the stack. Place the tin on the lower rack of the halogen oven.

Set the temperature to 225°C (437°F) and cook for about 10 minutes until the stacks are heated through and the mozzarella is soft. Transfer to serving plates, drizzle with balsamic vinegar and garnish with rocket or basil leaves. Serve as a starter or to accompany lamb dishes.

sweet potato jackets

Serves **4**

Preparation time **10 minutes**

Cooking time **50 minutes**

4 **sweet potatoes**, about
250 g (8 oz) each

25 g (1 oz) **butter**, melted

8 **spring onions**, finely
chopped

1 tablespoon finely chopped
oregano

1 tablespoon finely chopped
parsley

1 **garlic clove**, crushed

150 g (5 oz) **fresh goats'
cheese**

salt and **pepper**

finely chopped **lemon thyme**
or **coriander**, to garnish

Place the sweet potatoes on the lower rack of the
halogen oven. Brush with the butter and season lightly
with salt and pepper.

Set the temperature to 250°C (482°F) and cook for
about 40 minutes until tender. Leave until cool enough
to handle, then cut in half lengthways and scoop the
flesh into a bowl, leaving a 5 mm (¼ inch) thick shell.
Mash the flesh with a potato masher until smooth.

Add the spring onions, oregano, parsley, garlic, goats'
cheese, any remaining butter and plenty of pepper to
the bowl and mix well. Pile back into the shells.

Return to the lower rack of the oven and bake for a
further 10 minutes or until very hot. Serve as a light
lunch scattered with finely chopped lemon thyme or
coriander to garnish.

For crispy bacon & sweetcorn jackets, bake 4 floury
potatoes, about 250 g (8 oz) each, as above, increasing
the cooking time by about 10 minutes if they are still a
little firm. While cooking, finely chop 6 rindless streaky
bacon rashers and fry in 1 tablespoon vegetable oil
until crispy. Scoop out the potato from the shells,
leaving a 5 mm (¼ inch) thick shell, and mash in a
bowl. Cook 125 g (4 oz) sweetcorn and stir into the
mash along with 100 g (3½ oz) grated mature Cheddar
cheese, 2 tablespoons wholegrain mustard, 25 g
(1 oz) butter and the bacon. Pile back into the shells
and scatter with a further 25 g (1 oz) grated Cheddar
cheese. Finish cooking as above.

chilli parsnip chips & soured cream

Serves **4**

Preparation time **10 minutes**

Cooking time **25 minutes**

500 g (1 lb) small **parsnips**, cut lengthways into quarters

3 tablespoons **vegetable oil**

1 teaspoon **ground cumin**

1 teaspoon **ground coriander**

½ teaspoon **celery salt**

4 tablespoons **sweet chilli sauce**

Put the parsnips in a bowl. In a separate small bowl or jug, mix together the oil, cumin, coriander and celery salt. Add to the parsnips and mix well, turning the parsnips until they are evenly coated. Scatter in a shallow roasting tin and place on the upper rack of the halogen oven.

Set the temperature to 250°C (482°F) and cook for about 20 minutes, turning the parsnips frequently, until tender and turning golden. Brush with the chilli sauce and cook for a further 5 minutes.

Transfer to a serving bowl. Serve with soured cream for dipping as a snack or with pork or lamb chops.

For mushrooms with tarragon & cream, quarter 250 g (8 oz) chestnut mushrooms and toss with 25 g (1 oz) melted butter. Scatter in a shallow dish and season lightly with salt and pepper. Place on the upper rack of the halogen oven. Set the temperature to 250°C (482°F) and cook for 8 minutes, turning frequently. Melt a further 25 g (1 oz) butter and mix with 50 g (2 oz) fresh white breadcrumbs. Scatter 2 tablespoons chopped tarragon over the mushrooms and pour over 100 ml (3½ fl oz) single cream. Scatter with the breadcrumbs and cook for a further 5–10 minutes until heated through.

breads & baking

poppy seed bread

Makes **1 loaf**
Preparation time **15 minutes,**
   plus proving
Cooking time **30 minutes**

675 g (1 lb 6 oz) **strong white**
   flour, plus extra for dusting
2 teaspoons **easy-blend**
   dried yeast
1 teaspoon **salt**
1 teaspoon **caster sugar**
25 g (1 oz) **butter**, melted,
   plus extra for greasing
150 ml (¼ pint) **warm milk**,
   plus extra for brushing
300 ml (½ pint) **warm water**
vegetable oil, for oiling
poppy seeds, for sprinkling

Grease a large loaf tin. Put the flour, yeast, salt and sugar in a bowl. Mix the butter with the milk and the measurement water and add to the bowl. Mix with a round-bladed knife to make a soft but not sticky dough.

Turn the dough out on to a floured surface and knead for about 10 minutes until smooth and elastic. Place in a lightly oiled bowl, cover with clingfilm and leave to rise in a warm place for 1 hour or until doubled in size.

Tip the dough on to a floured surface and shape into an oval slightly shorter than the length of the tin. Drop into the tin and cover loosely with oiled clingfilm. Leave to rise for about 45 minutes until doubled in size. Brush the top of the loaf with a little milk and sprinkle with poppy seeds. Place on the lower rack of the halogen oven.

Set the temperature to 200°C (392°F) and cook for about 30 minutes until risen and deep golden, covering with foil if the surface starts to brown too much. Turn out of the tin and tap the bottom of the bread; if it sounds hollow, the bread is cooked. If needed, return to the oven (out of the tin) and cook a little longer.

For quick & easy soda bread, mix together 250 g (8 oz) self-raising flour, 250 g (8 oz) wholemeal flour, 1 teaspoon bicarbonate of soda and 1 teaspoon salt. Stir 1 tablespoon lemon juice into 275 ml (9 fl oz) milk and add to the bowl. Mix to a soft but not sticky dough, adding a dash more milk if it feels dry. Shape on a floured surface into a round. Place in a lightly greased shallow tin and flatten slightly. Brush with a little egg and dust with flour. Score a deep cross in the top and cook as above for about 25 minutes.

coriander & garlic naan

Makes **8**

Preparation time **25 minutes,
plus proving**

Cooking time **25 minutes**

650 g (1 lb 5 oz) **strong white
flour**, plus extra for dusting
1 teaspoon **salt**
1 teaspoon **caster sugar**
2 teaspoons **easy-blend
dried yeast**
75 g (3 oz) **butter**, plus extra
for greasing
handful of chopped **coriander**
2 **garlic cloves**, crushed
275 ml (9 fl oz) **warm milk**
2 tablespoons **natural yogurt**

Put the flour, salt, sugar and yeast in a large bowl.
Melt 50 g (2 oz) of the butter and stir in along with
the coriander, garlic, warm milk and yogurt. Mix with a
round-bladed knife to make a dough, adding a dash
more milk if the dough is crumbly.

Turn the dough out on to a floured surface and knead
for about 10 minutes until the dough is smooth and
elastic. Place in a lightly oiled bowl, cover with clingfilm
and leave to rise in a warm place for about 1 hour or
until doubled in size.

Tip the dough out on to a lightly floured surface and cut
into 8 even-sized pieces. Roll each into a ball, cover with
a clean tea towel and leave to stand for 10 minutes.
Thinly roll out each ball into a large teardrop shape and
place on a floured tray.

Melt the remaining butter and brush a little over 2 of
the breads. Transfer to a shallow greased baking sheet
and place on the upper rack of the halogen oven.

Set the temperature to 250°C (482°F) and cook for
about 6 minutes until puffed and golden. Stack on a
plate and cover with a tea towel while you cook the
remaining flat breads in the same way.

For seeded naan, crush 10 cardamom pods using a
mortar and pestle. Remove the husks and crush the
seeds as finely as possible. Add 2 teaspoons coriander
seeds and 2 teaspoons cumin seeds to the mortar
and crush again. Mix in with the dough ingredients
and make as above, sprinkling the breads with sesame
seeds after brushing with melted butter.

banana bread

Makes **10 slices**
Preparation time **15 minutes**
Cooking time **50 minutes**

2 large ripe **bananas**
100 g (3½ oz) lightly salted
    butter, softened, plus extra
    for greasing
75 g (3 oz) **light muscovado
    sugar**
100 ml (3½ fl oz) **maple syrup**
1 **egg**, beaten
150 ml (¼ pint) **Greek yogurt**
250 g (8 oz) **self-raising flour**
1 teaspoon **baking powder**
icing sugar, to dust

Grease a large loaf tin that will fit on the lower rack of the halogen oven. Mash the bananas.

Beat together the butter, sugar and maple syrup using a hand-held electric whisk until pale and creamy. Stir in the egg, yogurt and mashed banana until evenly combined. Sift the flour and baking powder into the bowl and stir in until just mixed through. Turn into the prepared tin and level the surface. Place on the lower rack of the halogen oven and cover with foil.

Set the temperature to 175°C (347°F) and cook for 35 minutes. Lift away the foil and cook for a further 15 minutes until risen and just firm to the touch. (A skewer inserted into the centre of the cake should come out clean.) Leave in the tin for 10 minutes, then transfer to a wire rack to cool. Serve dusted with icing sugar, cut into slices.

For pecan cake with maple butter, roughly chop 50 g (2 oz) pecan nuts. Make the cake mixture as above and stir in the nuts and 1 teaspoon ground mixed spice with the yogurt and mashed banana. While cooking, beat 100 g (3½ oz) softened lightly salted butter in a bowl with 75 ml (3 fl oz) maple syrup and 50 g (2 oz) icing sugar until combined. Chill until the cake has cooled, then spread over the top and scatter with extra pecan nuts.

summer fruits shortcake

Serves **8**
Preparation time **30 minutes**
Cooking time **25 minutes**

175 g (6 oz) **lightly salted butter**, softened, plus extra for greasing
100 g (3½ oz) **caster sugar**
1 teaspoon **vanilla extract**
2 **eggs**, beaten
225 g (7½ oz) **self-raising flour**
1 teaspoon **baking powder**

Filling
350g (11½ oz) **soft summer fruits**, such as strawberries, raspberries and redcurrants
300 ml (½ pint) **double cream**, lightly whipped
75 ml (3 fl oz) **redcurrant jelly**
1 tablespoon **water**

Grease a large loaf tin that will fit on the lower rack of the halogen oven. Line the bottom and long sides with a strip of greaseproof paper. Grease the paper.

Cream together the butter, sugar and vanilla using a hand-held electric whisk until light and fluffy. Gradually beat in the eggs. Sift the flour and baking powder into the bowl and stir in until just combined. Turn into the prepared tin and level the surface. Place on the lower rack of the halogen oven.

Set the temperature to 175°C (347°F) and cook for 25 minutes until risen and firm to the touch. Transfer to a wire rack to cool.

Hull the strawberries, halving any large ones, and mix with the other fruits. Lightly whip the cream. Melt the redcurrant jelly in a small saucepan with the measurement water until smooth. Split the cake in half horizontally and sandwich together with half the cream and fruits. Drizzle with half the redcurrant jelly. Position the top half of the cake and decorate with the remaining cream and fruit. Spoon over the remaining redcurrant jelly.

For tropical fruit shortcake, add 2 pieces of finely chopped stem ginger to the cake mixture and bake as above. Beat 250 g (8 oz) mascarpone cheese with 150 ml (¼ pint) double cream until just holding its shape. Press 75 ml (3 fl oz) ginger jam through a sieve to remove any pieces and heat in a small pan with 1 tablespoon water. Assemble the cake as above with 1 sliced mango and 1 sliced pineapple, the mascarpone cream and ginger jam.

garlic dipping sticks

Serves **6**
Preparation time **5 minutes**
Cooking time **15 minutes**

1 **part-baked ciabatta loaf**
4 **garlic cloves**, crushed
100 ml (3½ fl oz) **extra virgin olive oil**
sea salt, for sprinkling

Cut the bread in half widthways. Cut each half horizontally into 3 thin layers, then lengthways into 1 cm (½ inch) wide sticks.

Mix the garlic with the olive oil. Arrange the breadsticks slightly apart in a shallow roasting tin or on a baking sheet. Drizzle with a little of the garlic oil. (You will need to cook the bread in batches.) Place on the upper rack of the halogen oven and sprinkle with sea salt.

Set the temperature to 200°C (392°F) and cook for about 8 minutes until crisp and golden. Transfer to a wire rack while you cook the remainder. Serve with pre-dinner drinks or as a starter with cured meats, olives, roasted vegetables or other antipasto dishes.

For prosciutto-wrapped breadsticks, cut a part-baked olive ciabatta loaf into breadsticks as above. Mix 4 tablespoons olive oil with 1 teaspoon dried oregano, a little salt and ½ teaspoon freshly ground black pepper. Brush over the sticks. Cut 100 g (3½ oz) prosciutto into 2 cm (¾ inch) wide strips and wrap around the sticks. Cook as above.

garlic dip

Serves 6
Preparation time 5 minutes
Cooking time 15 minutes

sun-dried tomato bread

Serves **6**
Preparation time **20 minutes**
Cooking time **15 minutes**

75 g (3 oz) **lightly salted
  butter**, softened
6 **sun-dried tomatoes in oil**,
  finely drained and chopped
3 **garlic cloves**, crushed
finely grated rind of **1 lemon**
3 tablespoons chopped
  parsley
1 large **ciabatta loaf**
salt and **pepper**

Beat together the butter, tomatoes, garlic, lemon rind
and parsley with a little salt and pepper.

Make deep diagonal cuts, 2 cm (¾ inch) apart, down
the length of the bread, keeping the bread intact
underneath. Spread the flavoured butter into the cuts,
spreading any excess butter over the top of the bread.
Wrap in foil, with the opening along the top of the
bread, and place on the lower rack of the halogen oven.

Set the temperature to 250°C (482°F) and cook for
8–10 minutes until the butter has melted into the bread.
Open out the top of the foil and cook for a further
4–5 minutes until the surface is golden.

For roasted vegetable picnic loaf, core and deseed
4 red peppers then cut into large chunks. Put in the
bowl of the halogen oven with 2 large sliced courgettes
and 1 thinly sliced red onion. Drizzle with 3 tablespoons
olive oil and cook at 250°C (482°F) for about 40
minutes, stirring occasionally, until roasted. Remove a
shallow horizontal slice off the top of a ciabatta loaf
and scoop out the centre of the bread, leaving a 1 cm
(½ inch) shell. (Make breadcrumbs with the scooped-
out bread and freeze for another time.) Mix 3–4
tablespoons olive oil with 2 crushed garlic cloves and
brush over the inside of the bread. Pack half the roasted
vegetables into the centre, then scatter with 100 g
(3½ oz) feta cheese and a handful of chopped basil.
Layer the remaining vegetables on top and scatter with
another 100 g (3½ oz) feta and 2 tablespoons rinsed
and drained capers. Heat through on the lower rack of
the halogen oven for 10 minutes. Serve warm or cold
in slices.

iced cherry cupcakes

Makes **12**
Preparation time **15 minutes**
Cooking time **30 minutes**

150 g (5 oz) **lightly salted butter**, softened
150 g (5 oz) **caster sugar**
3 **eggs**
175 g (6 oz) **self-raising flour**
75 g (3 oz) **dried cherries**

Icing
150 g (5 oz) **icing sugar**
4–5 teaspoons **lemon juice**
12 **fresh cherries**, to decorate (optional)

Line a 6-hole muffin tray with paper cake cases.

Put the butter, caster sugar, eggs and flour in a bowl and beat together using a hand-held electric whisk until pale and creamy. Spoon half the mixture into the cake cases, reserving the remainder for cooking a second batch. Place on the lower rack of the halogen oven.

Set the temperature to 175°C (347°F) and cook for about 15 minutes until risen and just firm to the touch. Leave in the tin for 5 minutes, then transfer to a wire rack while you cook the remainder of the cupcakes. Leave to cool completely.

Mix the icing sugar with enough lemon juice to make a smooth glacé icing that almost holds its shape. Spread over the cakes and decorate each one with a fresh cherry if liked.

For passion fruit & lime cupcakes, make the sponge mixture as above, omitting the dried cherries and adding the finely grated rind of 2 limes. Bake as above. Whip 150 ml (¼ pint) double cream with 1 tablespoon caster sugar and 1 tablespoon lime juice until only just holding its shape. Pipe or spoon over the cakes. Scoop the pulp from 2 passion fruit and beat together with about 125 g (4 oz) icing sugar until smooth and thickly coating the back of the spoon. Drizzle over the tops of the cakes so that the icing runs slightly down the sides.

vanilla & white chocolate cupcakes

Makes **10–12**
Preparation time **20 minutes**
Cooking time **30 minutes**

125 g (4 oz) **lightly salted butter**, softened
175 g (6 oz) **caster sugar**
2 **eggs**
100 ml (3½ fl oz) **milk**
1 teaspoon **vanilla bean paste** or **extract**
25 g (1 oz) **plain flour**
100 g (3½ oz) **self-raising flour**

Icing
100 g (3½ oz) **cream cheese**
25 g (1 oz) **white chocolate**, melted
50 g (2 oz) **lightly salted butter**, softened
½ teaspoon **vanilla bean paste** or **extract**
250 g (8 oz) **icing sugar**, plus extra for dusting
white chocolate curls, to decorate

Line a 6-hole muffin tray with paper cake cases.

Cream together the butter and caster sugar using a hand-held electric whisk until light and fluffy. Beat in one egg, half the milk and the vanilla, then the plain flour. Stir in the remaining egg and milk. Add the self-raising flour, stirring until just combined. Use to fill the cake cases, reserving the excess to make a second batch. Place on the lower rack of the halogen oven.

Set the temperature to 200°C (392°F) and cook for about 15 minutes until risen and just firm to the touch. Leave in the tin for 5 minutes, then transfer to a wire rack while you cook the remaining mixture.

Make the icing. Put the cream cheese, chocolate, butter, vanilla and icing sugar in a bowl and beat until smooth and creamy. Spread over the tops of the cakes. Scatter with plenty of white chocolate curls and dust with extra icing sugar to decorate.

For chocolate fudge cupcakes, beat together 125 g (4 oz) softened lightly salted butter, 150 g (5 oz) dark muscovado sugar, 2 eggs, 100 g (3½ oz) self-raising flour, 50 g (2 oz) cocoa powder and ½ teaspoon baking powder. Divide among the paper cake cases and bake as above. To decorate, put 100 g (3½ oz) chopped milk chocolate, 2 tablespoons milk and 50 g (2 oz) lightly salted butter in a bowl set over a saucepan of simmering water and heat gently until smooth. Tip into a bowl and stir in 75 g (3 oz) icing sugar until smooth. Spread over the cupcakes.

blueberry & apple slice

Makes **8 slices**
Preparation time **20 minutes**
Cooking time **45 minutes**

225 g (7½ oz) **self-raising flour**
125 g (4 oz) firm **lightly salted butter**, cut into small pieces, plus extra for greasing
175 g (6 oz) **caster sugar**
2 **eggs**
4 tablespoons **milk**
2 **crisp dessert apples**, peeled, cored and thinly sliced
125 g (4 oz) **blueberries**
vanilla sugar, for sprinkling

Grease a large loaf tin that will fit on the lower rack of the halogen oven. Line the bottom and long sides with a strip of greaseproof paper. Grease the paper.

Put the flour and butter in a food processor. Process until the mixture resembles fine breadcrumbs. Add the sugar, eggs and milk and process to a dough.

Spread half the cake mixture into the loaf tin and scatter with half the apples and blueberries. Spread the remaining cake mixture over the top, then scatter with the remaining fruits. Place on the lower rack of the halogen oven.

Set the temperature to 200°C (392°F) and cook for about 45 minutes, covering with foil if the surface starts to brown too much, until a skewer inserted into the centre comes out clean. Leave in the tin for 10 minutes, then transfer to a plate or board. Sprinke with vanilla sugar and serve warm, in slices, with clotted cream.

For lemon & raspberry slice, prepare the loaf tin and sponge cake as above, omitting the apples and blueberries, and adding the finely grated rind of 1 lemon. Bake as above. Once cool, split the cake in half horizontally. Whip 150 ml (¼ pint) double cream until peaks form and spread over the lower half of the cake. Drizzle with 75 ml (3 fl oz) lemon curd and scatter with 200 g (7 oz) raspberries. Position the second cake layer on top and dust generously with icing sugar.

desserts &
puddings

summer fruit & pear betty

Serves **4–6**
Preparation time **15 minutes**
Cooking time **30 minutes**

350 g (11½ oz) **mixed
summer fruits,** such as
strawberries, raspberries,
blackcurrants or redcurrants
and blackberries
3 tablespoons **light
muscovado sugar**
4 tablespoons **raspberry** or
strawberry conserve
6 ripe **pears**
50 g (2 oz) **fresh white
breadcrumbs**
25 g (1 oz) **butter,** melted
4 tablespoons lightly toasted
flaked almonds

Put the summer fruits in a bowl and sprinkle over the sugar. Dot with the conserve and stir the ingredients together until evenly mixed. Peel, core and quarter the pears, add to the summer fruits and mix in lightly.

Tip the fruit mixture into an ovenproof dish, cover with foil and place on the lower rack of the halogen oven.

Set the temperature to 250°C (482°F) and cook for 15–20 minutes until the pears are tender. (The cooking time will depend on the ripeness of the pears.)

Meanwhile, stir together the breadcrumbs, melted butter and almonds, and sprinkle over the fruit. Reduce the oven temperature to 200°C (392°F) and cook, uncovered, for a further 10 minutes or until the top is golden. Serve warm with vanilla custard (see page 220).

For apple, blackberry & ginger betty, make the recipe as above, but using 350 g (11½ oz) blackberries, 3 small peeled, cored and chopped cooking apples and 4 tablespoons blackberry conserve or jam instead of the summer fruits, pears and raspberry or strawberry conserve. Extend the cooking time by 10 minutes to soften the cooking apples. For the topping, finely grate 40 g (1½ oz) fresh root ginger and mix with the melted butter before stirring with the breadcrumbs. Finish as above.

cinnamon apple crunch

Serves **6**

Preparation time **20 minutes**

Cooking time **40 minutes**

1 kg (2 lb) **cooking apples**

75 g (3 oz) **caster sugar**

1 tablespoon **lemon juice**

100 g (3½ oz) **unsalted butter**

1 teaspoon **ground cinnamon**

200 g (7 oz) **porridge oats**

50 g (2 oz) **light muscovado sugar**

Peel, core and slice the apples, then scatter over the bottom of a shallow ovenproof dish and sprinkle with the caster sugar. Drizzle with the lemon juice.

Melt the butter in a saucepan on the hob and stir in the cinnamon, then the oats and muscovado sugar until evenly mixed. Spoon the mixture over the apples. Cover the dish with foil and place on the lower rack of the halogen oven.

Set the temperature to 200°C (392°F) and cook for 40 minutes, removing the foil for the final 10 minutes of cooking time to colour the crumble topping. Serve with vanilla ice cream.

For summer fruit & granola crumbles, scatter 500 g (1 lb) mixed summer fruits into a shallow ovenproof dish and sprinkle with 25 g (1 oz) caster sugar. In a food processor, process 50 g (2 oz) unsalted butter with 50 g (2 oz) plain flour until the mixture resembles fine breadcrumbs. Add 150 g (5 oz) granola and 75 g (3 oz) caster sugar. Process briefly until the cereal is broken up. Spoon over the fruits and bake as above.

jam roly-poly

Serves **3–4**
Preparation time **15 minutes**
Cooking time **1 hour**

100 g (3½ oz) **self-raising flour**, plus extra for dusting
pinch of **salt**
50 g (2 oz) **shredded vegetable** or **beef suet**
1 tablespoon **caster sugar**, plus extra for sprinkling
2–3 tablespoons **water**
75 ml (3 fl oz) **raspberry** or **strawberry jam**
milk, for brushing
butter, for greasing

Put the flour, salt, suet and the sugar in a bowl. Stir in enough of the measurement water to mix to a soft but not sticky dough. Turn the dough out on to a floured surface and roll out to a rectangle about 19 cm x 15 cm (7 ½ inches x 6 inches) and about 5 mm (¼ inch) thick.

Spread 3 tablespoons of the jam over the dough to about 1 cm (½ inch) away from the edges. Brush the edges with milk and roll up the dough, starting from a short end. Pinch the ends firmly together to seal. Wrap loosely in greased foil and place on the upper rack of the halogen oven. Brush with a little more milk and sprinkle with extra sugar.

Pour boiling water to a depth of 3 cm (1 ¼ inches) into the bowl of the halogen oven. Set the temperature to 150°C (302°F) and cook the roly-poly for 1 hour until golden, covering with foil if the top starts to brown too much. Transfer to a serving plate.

Warm the remaining jam in a small saucepan and drizzle over the pudding. Serve with vanilla custard.

For homemade vanilla custard, whisk 3 egg yolks in a heatproof bowl with 15 g (½ oz) caster sugar and 1 teaspoon vanilla bean paste or extract. Pour 150 ml (¼ pint) milk and 150 ml (¼ pint) single cream into a saucepan and heat until almost boiling. Pour over the egg yolk mixture, stirring. Return the mixture to the cleaned pan and cook over a gentle heat, stirring continuously, until the custard thinly coats the back of the spoon. Take care not to overheat the custard or it will separate. Pour into a jug and serve.

pistachio & chocolate torte

Serves **4–6**
Preparation time **20 minutes**
Cooking time **25 minutes**

50 g (2 oz) **unsalted shelled
    pistachio nuts**, plus extra
    2 tablespoons, skinned
    and roughly chopped, to
    decorate
125 g (4 oz) **lightly salted
    butter**, softened
125 g (4 oz) **caster sugar**
100 g (3½ oz) **self-raising
    flour**
40 g (1½ oz) **cocoa powder**,
    plus extra for dusting
1½ teaspoons **baking powder**
2 **eggs**, beaten
4 tablespoons **milk**
75 g (3 oz) **plain dark** or **milk
    chocolate**, chopped

Grind the pistachio nuts in a food processor. Grease a 20 cm (8 inch) sandwich tin or springform tin. Line the bottom with greaseproof paper.

Cream together the butter and sugar until smooth and creamy. Beat in the ground pistachio nuts, flour, cocoa powder, baking powder, eggs and milk. Mix until evenly combined.

Pour the mixture into the prepared cake tin and spread in an even layer. Scatter the chocolate pieces and extra chopped pistachio nuts over the top and place on the lower rack of the halogen oven.

Set the temperature to 175°C (347°F) and cook for about 25 minutes until the top feels firm to the touch. (A skewer inserted into the centre should come out slightly moist.) Leave to cool in the tin for 10 minutes before transferring to a plate. Dust with extra cocoa powder and serve warm with lightly whipped cream.

For amaretti & almond torte, grind 50 g (2 oz) blanched almonds in a food processor. Tip into a bowl and crush 40 g (1½ oz) amaretti biscuits in the machine. Make the sponge as above, replacing the pistachio nuts with the almonds and the cocoa powder with the crushed amaretti. Scatter 75 g (3 oz) dried sour cherries over the top instead of the chocolate. Cook as above, covering with foil if the top starts to brown too much. Serve with crème fraîche.

sultana lemon pudding

Serves **4–5**
Preparation time **15 minutes**
Cooking time **30 minutes**

150 g (5 oz) **caster sugar**
75 g (3 oz) **plain flour**
350 ml (12 fl oz) **full-cream**
 or **semi-skimmed milk**
75 g (3 oz) **lightly salted**
 butter, melted
3 **eggs**, separated
finely grated rind of 2 **lemons**,
 plus 90 ml (3½ fl oz) juice
3 tablespoons **sultanas**

Put 125 g (4 oz) of the sugar in a bowl with the flour. Warm the milk in a small saucepan on the hob and mix with the melted butter and egg yolks. Add to the dry ingredients along with the lemon rind and juice. Whisk well to mix.

Whisk the egg whites in a thoroughly clean, dry bowl until soft peaks form. Gradually whisk in the remaining sugar, a tablespoonful at a time, until the mixture is smooth and glossy. Whisk a quarter of the whisked whites into the lemon mixture to lighten it, then stir in the remainder.

Scatter the sultanas over the bottom of an ovenproof dish and pour the lemon mixture over the top. Place the dish on the lower rack of the halogen oven. Carefully pour hot water into the bowl of the halogen oven until it comes slightly up the sides of the dish.

Set the temperature to 175°C (347°F) and cook for 30 minutes until the pudding feels spongy on the top but is quite syrupy on the bottom. (Test by inserting the tip of a knife down the side of the pudding.) Serve with lightly whipped cream or crème fraîche.

For blueberry & orange pudding, scatter 200 g (7 oz) blueberries over the bottom of an ovenproof dish and drizzle with 3 tablespoons orange liqueur. Make the pudding mixture as above using the rind of 1 orange instead of the lemon rind and replacing the lemon juice with 3 tablespoons orange juice. Cook as above.

chocolate & cranberry cookies

Makes **20 cookies**
Preparation time **15 minutes**
Cooking time **20 minutes**

125 g (4oz) **lightly salted
  butter**, softened, plus extra
  for greasing
125 g (4 oz) **light muscovado
  sugar**
1 **egg**
1 teaspoon **vanilla extract**
150 g (5 oz) **plain flour**
½ teaspoon **baking powder**
50 g (2 oz) **dried cranberries**
100 g (3½ oz) good-quality
  white chocolate, chopped
  into small pieces

Beat together the butter, sugar, egg, vanilla, flour and baking powder until evenly mixed. Stir in the cranberries and chopped chocolate.

Take heaped teaspoons of the cookie mixture and space them well apart in a greased shallow roasting tin or on a baking sheet, as the cookies will spread quite a bit when cooking. (You will need to cook the mixture in 2 batches.) Place the tin or sheet on the upper rack of the halogen oven.

Set the temperature to 175°C (347°F) and bake for 10 minutes. Leave to cool slightly, then transfer to a wire rack and cook the remainder of the mixture in the same way.

For rich chocolate cookies, make the cookie mixture as above, replacing 25 g (1 oz) of the flour with the same amount of cocoa powder. Use 150 g (5 oz) chopped plain dark chocolate to replace the cranberries and white chocolate. After baking, drizzle lines of melted milk chocolate back and forth across the cookies to decorate.

poached pears in ginger wine

Serves **4**
Preparation time **15 minutes**
Cooking time **35 minutes**

4 **firm dessert pears**
1 tablespoon **lemon juice**
300 ml (½ pint) **ginger wine**
50 g (2 oz) **caster sugar**
1 **cinnamon stick**, halved

Peel the pears, leaving the stalks attached, and brush with the lemon juice to prevent discoloration. Pour the wine into a shallow ovenproof dish and place on the lower rack of the halogen oven.

Set the temperature to 250°C (482°F) and cook for about 5 minutes until hot. Stir in the sugar, then carefully add the pears and cinnamon. Reduce the heat to 150°C (302°F) and cook for 25–30 minutes until the pears are tender. (The cooking time will vary slightly depending on the ripeness of the pears.) Turn and baste the pears with the wine a couple of times during cooking.

Transfer the pears to small serving dishes and spoon over the syrup. Serve warm with vanilla ice cream.

For poached pears with chocolate sauce, prepare and cook the pears as above, using 300 ml (½ pint) white wine instead of the ginger wine. To make the chocolate sauce, put 125 g (4 oz) caster sugar in a small saucepan with 125 ml (4 fl oz) water. Heat gently until the sugar has dissolved. Boil the syrup for 1 minute, then remove from the heat and leave to cool slightly. Stir in 200 g (7 oz) chopped plain dark chocolate and 25 g (1 oz) unsalted butter. Stir until the chocolate and butter melt to make a smooth sauce. Return to a very gentle heat if needed, to ensure that all the chocolate has melted.

honeyed bread & butter pudding

Serves **4**

Preparation time **15 minutes, plus standing**

Cooking time **40 minutes**

50 g (2 oz) **unsalted butter**, softened, plus extra for greasing

4 thin slices good-quality **white bread**

100 g (3½ oz) **raisins**

2 **eggs**

1 **egg yolk**

finely grated rind of 1 **lemon**

275 ml (9 fl oz) **full-cream** or **semi-skimmed milk**

25 g (1 oz) **caster sugar**

3 tablespoons **clear honey**, plus extra to serve (optional)

freshly grated **nutmeg**

Butter the slices of bread generously with the softened butter and cut into triangles. Grease a shallow pie dish and arrange the bread slices in the dish, sprinkling the layers with the raisins.

Beat together the eggs and egg yolk in a jug. Whisk in the lemon rind, milk, sugar and honey. Pour the custard over the bread and leave to stand for 1 hour.

Sprinkle the top of the pudding with plenty of freshly grated nutmeg. Place the pie on the lower rack of the halogen oven.

Set the temperature to 150°C (302°F) and cook the pudding for 35–40 minutes until the top is golden and the custard lightly set. If needed, cover the pudding with foil if the top starts to brown too much. Drizzle with extra honey, if liked, and serve warm with pouring cream.

For cinnamon & date pudding, instead of the raisins chop 100 g (3½ oz) plump pitted dates into small pieces. Butter and layer up the bread slices as above, scattering the dates in between. Make the custard as above, adding 1 teaspoon rosewater and ¼ teaspoon ground cinnamon. Finish as above.

frosted carrot cake

Makes **9 squares**
Preparation time **20 minutes**
Cooking time **30 minutes**

125 ml (4 fl oz) **sunflower oil**,
plus extra for oiling
125 g (4 oz) **light muscovado
sugar**
2 **eggs**
125 g (4 oz) **self-raising flour**
1 teaspoon **ground mixed
spice**
125 g (4 oz) **carrots**, coarsely
grated
25 g (1 oz) **sultanas**

Cream cheese frosting
100 g (3½ oz) **full-fat cream
cheese**
½ teaspoon **vanilla extract**
75 g (3 oz) **icing sugar**

Oil an 18 cm (7 inch) square cake tin and line with greaseproof paper. Oil the paper.

Whisk together the oil and muscovado sugar to combine, then whisk in the eggs. Sift the flour and mixed spice into the bowl and stir in. Add the carrots and sultanas, and mix well. Pour the mixture into the tin and level the top. Place on the lower rack of the halogen oven.

Set the temperature to 175°C (347°F) and cook for about 30 minutes until just firm to the touch. Leave in the tin for 10 minutes, then transfer to a wire rack to cool.

Beat together the cream cheese, vanilla and icing sugar to make the frosting. Spread over the cooled cake with a palette knife. Serve cut into squares.

For walnut & apple slice, peel and core 2 small apples and coarsely grate the flesh. Pat dry between several sheets of kitchen paper. Roughly chop 75 g (3 oz) walnuts. Make the cake as above, using the apples and walnuts instead of the carrots and sultanas, and adding ½ teaspoon ground cinnamon to the mixture. Bake as above and serve warm with crème fraîche, or leave to cool and spread with cream cheese frosting as above.

syrup sponge pudding

Serves **4**
Preparation time **15 minutes**
Cooking time **1 hour**
  30 minutes

butter, for greasing
75 ml (3 fl oz) **golden syrup**,
  plus extra to serve
175 g (6 oz) **self-raising flour**
75 g (3 oz) **shredded**
  vegetable or **beef suet**
50 g (2 oz) **caster sugar**
1 **egg**, beaten
100 ml (3½ fl oz) **milk**

Grease a 1 litre (1¾ pint) pudding basin and line the inside with a circle of greaseproof paper. Spoon the 75 ml (3 fl oz) golden syrup into the basin.

Mix together the flour, suet and sugar in a bowl. Stir in the egg and milk until thoroughly combined. Spoon the mixture into the basin and level the top.

Cover the basin with a double layer of baking parchment, securing around the rim with kitchen string. Cover with foil, scrunching it over the paper tightly to seal. Sit the pudding basin in the bowl of the halogen oven and pour in enough boiling water to come a third of the way up the side of the basin.

Set the temperature to 250°C (482°F) and steam the pudding for 1½–1¾ hours until the top of the pudding feels just firm to the touch and a knife inserted into the centre comes out clean. Leave in the basin for 5 minutes, then invert on to a serving plate and peel away the lining paper. Serve with warm vanilla custard (see page 220) and extra syrup for drizzling over.

For ginger spice pudding, line the basin as above, then add 75 ml (3 fl oz) ginger marmalade instead of the syrup. Finely chop 50 g (2 oz) preserved stem ginger from a jar. Make the pudding mixture as above, stirring the chopped stem ginger, 1 teaspoon ground mixed spice and 50 g (2 oz) sultanas into the dry ingredients. Turn into the basin and cook as above. Serve with crème fraîche.

index

acknowledgements

Consulting editor: Joanna Farrow
Commissioning editor: Eleanor Maxfield
Editor: Jo Wilson
Executive art editor: Karen Sawyer
Designer: Sally Bond
Photographer: William Shaw
Home economist: Denise Smart, Sue Henderson
Props stylist: Liz Hippisley
Production controller: Caroline Alberti

Other photography: © Octopus Publishing Group/Stephen Conroy 38, 174, 214; /Ian Garlick 10, 11, 12, 13, 14, 15, 37, 43, 61, 81, 87, 105, 111, 163, 167, 217; /David Munns 16; / Lis Parsons 84, 108, 130, 150, 194; /Ian Wallace 62
All other photography: © Octopus Publishing Group Limited/ William Shaw